W9-BIP-252

Microsoft®
FrontPage 98
At a Glance

Microsoft®Press

Published by **Microsoft Press**
A Division of Microsoft Corporation
One Microsoft Way
Redmond, Washington 98052-6399

Nelson, Stephen L., 1959–
    Microsoft FrontPage 98 at a glance / Stephen L. Nelson.
          p. cm.
    Includes index.
    ISBN 1-57231-637-3
    1. Microsoft FrontPage. 2. Web sites--Design. 3. Web Publishing.
I. Title.
TK5105.8885.F76N45 1997
005.7'2--dc21   97-33676
             CIP

Printed and bound in the United States of America.

2 3 4 5 6 7 8 9   QEQE   2 1 0 9 8

Distributed to the book trade in Canada by Macmillan of Canada, a division of Canada Publishing Corporation.

A CIP catalogue record for this book is available from the British Library.

Microsoft Press books are available through booksellers and distributors worldwide. For further information about international editions, contact your local Microsoft Corporation office. Or contact Microsoft Press International directly at fax (206) 936-7329.

For Stephen L. Nelson, Inc.
Writers: **Steve Nelson, Kaarin Dolliver**
Editor: **Paula Thurman**
Technical Editor: **Jason Gerend**

For Microsoft Press
Acquisitions Editor: **Kim Fryer**
Project Editor: **Lucinda Rowley**

Contents

View how your web pages
link together
see pages 16–17

*How can I
remove a web
page from the
site?*

see page 28

How do I spell check my web pages?

see page 44

Add a hyperlink to an image
see pages 74–75

*How do I save
all the web pages
in a web site?*

see page 97

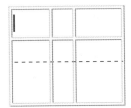

Draw a table
see page 101

How do I change the frames page grid?

see page 130

Apply Now

Insert a hover buttton
see page 150

Add a page banner
see page 160

*How do I
add choices to a
drop-down menu
form field?*

see page 181

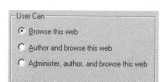

Change user permissions
for a web site
see page 201

About This Book

Microsoft *FrontPage 98 At a Glance* is for anyone who wants to begin web publishing with Microsoft FrontPage 98. You'll find this book to be a straightforward, easy-to-read reference tool. With the premise that web publishing isn't something only the experts can (or should) do, this book's purpose is to help you get your work done quickly and efficiently so that you can focus your web publishing efforts on the most important and more enjoyable parts of web publishing: finding, packaging, and presenting interesting or useful information.

No Computerese!

Let's face it—when there's a task you don't know how to do but you need to get it done in a hurry or when you're stuck in the middle of a task and can't figure out what to do next, there's nothing more frustrating than having to read page after page of technical background material. You want the information you need—nothing more, nothing less—and you want it now! *And* it should be easy to find and understand.

That's what this book is all about. It's written in plain English—no technical jargon and no computerese. There's no single task in the book that takes more than two pages. (And most take a page or less.) Just look up the task in the index or the table of contents, turn to the page, and there's the information, laid out step by step and accompanied by a graphic image or two to add visual clarity. You don't get bogged down by the whys and wherefores: just follow the steps, look at the illustrations, and get your work done with a minimum of hassle.

Occasionally you might have to turn to another page if the procedure you're working on has a "See Also" in the left column. That's because there's a lot of overlap among tasks, and I didn't want to keep repeating myself. I also scattered some useful tips here and there, and threw in a "Try This" once in a while, but by and large I tried to remain true to the heart and soul of the book, which is that the information you need should be available to you at a glance.

Useful Tasks…

Whether you use FrontPage for web publishing on the Internet or an intranet, I've tried to pack this book with procedures for everything that you might want to do, from the simplest tasks to some of the more esoteric ones.

…And the Easiest Way To Do Them

Another thing I've tried to do in *Microsoft FrontPage 98 At a Glance* is to find and document the easiest way to accomplish a task. FrontPage often provides a multitude of methods to accomplish a single end result, which can be daunting or delightful, depending on the way you like to work. If you tend to stick with one favorite and familiar approach, the methods described in this book are the way to go. If you like trying out alternative techniques, go ahead! The intuitiveness of FrontPage invites exploration, and you're likely to discover ways of doing things that you think are easier or that you like better than those presented here. If you do, that's great! It's exactly what the creators of FrontPage had in mind when they provided so many alternatives.

A Quick Overview

This book isn't meant to be read in any particular order. It's designed so that you can jump in, get the information you need, and then close the book and keep it near your computer until the next time you need to know how to get something done. But that doesn't mean I scattered the information about with wild abandon. If you were to read the book from front to back, you'd find a logical progression from the simple tasks to the more complex ones. Here's a quick overview.

You'll probably turn first to Sections 2 and 3. Section 2 tells how Microsoft FrontPage Explorer works and how you use it to describe in general terms an Internet or intranet web site you want to create. (FrontPage Explorer is one of the principal programs that comes in the FrontPage box.) Section 3 explains how you create and add text to your web pages using Microsoft FrontPage Editor. (FrontPage Editor is another principal program that comes in the FrontPage box.)

Section 4 explains how to incorporate graphic content into your web pages. It describes how you place graphic images in your web pages using FrontPage Editor.

Section 5 goes into more detail about how you work with FrontPage Editor. It talks in depth about how you manipulate and manage web pages, print them, save them, and how you perform many other tasks as well.

The remaining five sections of this book delve into an eclectic set of more advanced web publishing topics: Section 6, for example, explains how you add tables to your web pages, and Section 7 explains how you work with frames. Section 8 describes how you can use special effects—such as background sounds, video clips, and marquees—in your web pages. Section 9 tells you how to use FrontPage Components for your web site; Section 10 explains how you use forms; and, last but not least, Section 11 describes how you administer a web site.

Some Final Words

Let me close this introductory section with some final comments—comments, I hope, that you'll find helpful and encouraging as you use this book and learn FrontPage:

Whatever you *want* to do, this book helps you get it done.

This book helps you discover how to do things you *didn't* know you wanted to do.

And, finally, this book helps you *enjoy* your web publishing with FrontPage.

I hope you'll have as much fun using *Microsoft FrontPage 98 At a Glance* as I did writing it. The best way to learn is by *doing*, and that's what you'll get from this book.

Jump right in!

Creating a Web Site

Microsoft FrontPage, which is really a collection of programs, helps you create and administer web sites. This section describes how you use Microsoft FrontPage Explorer, one of the FrontPage programs, to create and work with web sites in FrontPage. The following sections provide step-by-step instructions for creating the web page documents that make up a web site. If the terms *web site* and *web page* are unfamiliar to you, read the "What Is a World Wide Web Site?" sidebar on page 7. It provides useful background information on the World Wide Web.

This section is designed to help you get comfortable navigating with FrontPage Explorer, a program you might initially find strange and confusing if you're used to working with word processing programs or even other Microsoft products. Whereas with many software programs, you start by opening a blank document and then filling it with information, in FrontPage you don't start out by creating individual web page documents. Instead, you describe in general terms the collection of web pages you want to create. Once you have created this web site, which FrontPage calls simply a web, you can begin entering content in individual web pages.

Getting Started with FrontPage Explorer

Start FrontPage Explorer to begin working with your first web site. You can use FrontPage Explorer to create a new web site, either from scratch or by using one of the web site wizards, or to open existing web sites.

FrontPage Explorer

Start FrontPage Explorer

1 Click the Start button.

2 Choose the Programs menu's Microsoft FrontPage command.

3 To open an existing web site (one you've already created), click the Open An Existing FrontPage Web option button and select the web you want to open from the list box.

4 To create a new web site, click the Create A New FrontPage Web option button.

5 After you've made your choice, click OK.

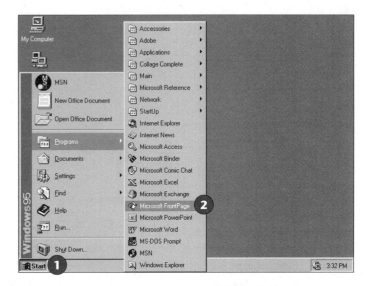

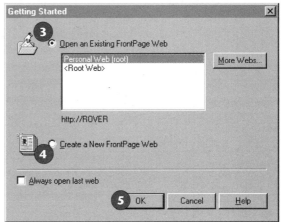

What Is a World Wide Web Site?

The World Wide Web (also known as W^3, the Web, and WWW) is just a set of multimedia documents that are connected by way of hyperlinks so that you can jump from one document to another, usually with a mouse click. If this definition sounds complicated, it's probably because I've used a handful of terms you might not know: documents, multimedia, and hyperlinks. Let me define these terms for you and clear up the picture.

Let's start with the key term, *document*. A document is just a report that describes something. Often, documents are on paper. In fact, you've probably created hundreds of paper documents: book reports in grade school; thank-you letters to distant, gift-giving relatives; and perhaps lengthy term papers in college. You wrote these documents on paper, but if you had produced and displayed them on a computer screen, they still would have been documents. So now you know what I mean by document.

The *multimedia* part relates to the fact that when you create and display a document on a computer, you aren't limited to words. You can place pictures in a document, for example. And you can place sounds in documents as well. (A World Wide Web document from the Office of the President of the United States plays Socks the cat's meow.) Just about any object a computer can create, display, or play can be placed in a document. So now you know what I mean by multimedia.

And now we come to what makes the World Wide Web unique—the *hyperlink* part. Hyperlinks are connections that let you jump from one document to another. Suppose, for example, that you're reading a document about the U.S. Department of Commerce and what it does. This document references, let's say, the Office of the President, with a hyperlink. You click on the words *Office of the President* and see a new document that talks about the president.

So to return to my original definition, the World Wide Web is simply a set of multimedia documents that are connected using hyperlinks. By clicking on the hyperlinks, you can jump from one document to another.

To view a World Wide Web document, you need to have a web browser such as Microsoft Internet Explorer. The documents you read, or view, with a web browser are written using something called HTML instructions. In fact, the web browser uses HTML instructions to display a document on your screen. The HTML instructions also include, in the case of the hyperlinks, uniform resource locators, or URLs, which describe the precise addresses of other HTML documents.

2

Creating a New Web Site

If you haven't already created the web site you want to work with in FrontPage, you need to do so first. While the notion of creating a conglomeration of linked pages might seem like a daunting task, FrontPage's wizards and templates make this step a simple one.

TIP

Getting to the New FrontPage Web dialog box. *If the Getting Started dialog box isn't showing, choose the File menu's New command to display the New submenu; then choose the New submenu's FrontPage Web command. FrontPage Explorer displays the New FrontPage Web dialog box.*

TIP

By default, FrontPage stores the new webs you create on the Personal Web Server on your computer. If you want to store a web somewhere else as you're working on it, you can enter a local pathname or a World Wide Web URL.

Create a New Web Site Using a Wizard

1 In the Getting Started dialog box, click the Create A New FrontPage Web option button. Then click OK.

2 Click the From Wizard Or Template option button, and select a wizard from the list box.

3 Type a name for the web site.

4 Optionally, click the Change button to specify a different location for the new web.

5 Check the Secure Connection Required (SSL) box if your server uses the special, secured https:// protocol.

6 Click OK to return to the New FrontPage Web dialog box.

7 Click OK to start the Web Site Wizard.

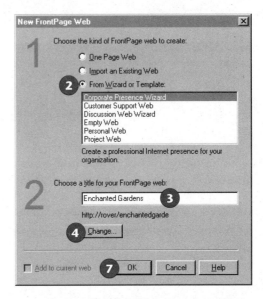

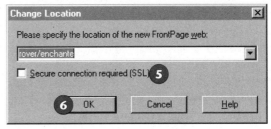

TIP

If FrontPage Explorer asks whether it can convert the folder you've selected to a FrontPage Web folder, click OK. For this conversion, FrontPage Explorer copies files it needs to the folder.

SEE ALSO

To learn more about FrontPage wizards, read the "Using FrontPage Web Wizards" sidebar on page 12.

TIP

If you want to add a new web to an existing web, open the web to which you want to add a new web and check the Add To Current Web box in the New FrontPage Web dialog box.

Create a New Web Site Using a Template

1 In the Getting Started dialog box, click the Create A New FrontPage Web option button. Then click OK.

2 Click the From Wizard Or Template option button, and select a template from the list box.

3 Type a name for the web site.

4 Optionally, click the Change button to specify a different location for the new web.

5 Check the Secure Connection Required (SSL) box if your server uses the special, secured https:// protocol.

6 Click OK to return to the New FrontPage Web dialog box.

7 Click OK. FrontPage Explorer creates a web site based on the template you chose.

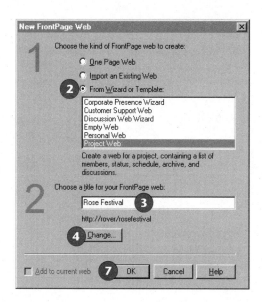

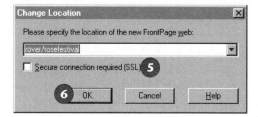

Opening a Web Site

Once you have a web site created, you need to open the web site to begin working on it each time you start FrontPage.

TIP

If the Getting Started dialog box isn't displayed, close any open web site.

Open an Existing Web Site

1 In the Getting Started dialog box, click the Open An Existing FrontPage Web option button.

2 Select the web you want to open from the list box, or click the More Webs button to open a web you've never opened before.

3 Click OK. FrontPage Explorer opens the web site.

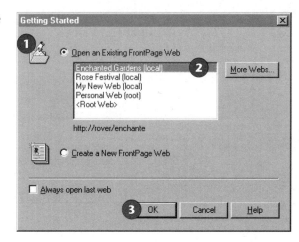

Finishing a FrontPage Session

When you are done working with a web site, you might want to close the site so that you can open a different site (because you can view only one web site at a time in FrontPage), or you might want to exit FrontPage altogether so that you can shut down your computer or free memory to use another program. Both of these tasks can be quickly and easily accomplished in FrontPage.

TRY THIS

Quick exit. *You can also exit FrontPage Explorer by clicking the application window's Close button. (The Close button is the button marked with an "X" in the upper-right corner of the application window.)*

Close a Web Site

1 Choose the File menu's Close FrontPage Web command.

Exit FrontPage Explorer

1 Choose the File menu's Exit command.

Using FrontPage Web Wizards

FrontPage Explorer's web wizards make it easy for you to create web sites. As you learned earlier in this section, these wizards ask you a series of questions by using buttons and boxes in dialog boxes. You answer the questions by clicking the buttons and entering information in the boxes. If you've never used a wizard, you may want to read about what happens when you run one.

Describe the Web Pages You Want

The first dialog box displayed by a web wizard states that you've started a web wizard, and it alerts you that you'll be asked a series of questions about what you want your web site to look like. To continue, you click the Next button. (While you're running the wizard, you can click the Next and Back buttons to move ahead to the next web wizard dialog box or back to the previous web wizard dialog box.)

The real action begins with the second web wizard dialog box. It asks which pages you want to include by using a list of check boxes, as shown in the following figure. You choose which pages you want by checking the appropriate boxes. If you don't know whether you want a particular page or not, go ahead and accept the wizard's initial, or suggested, setting. If you decide later that you've made a mistake, it's easy to add or remove a page.

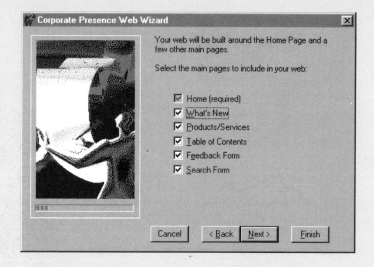

Explain How You Want Your Web Pages Organized

After you indicate which pages you want included in your web site, the wizard asks about—well, actually suggests— sections for the pages you've selected. In essence, by answering this set of questions, you partially describe how you want your web pages organized. For example, you'll be asked about what sections you want on your web site's Home page. And you'll be asked about what sections you want on your What's New page.

Provide Any Standard Page Information

Once you've described the pages you want and how you want them organized, the wizard asks what information you want to include on each and every page. As elsewhere in the wizard's dialog boxes, you specify what you want the wizard to do by checking boxes.

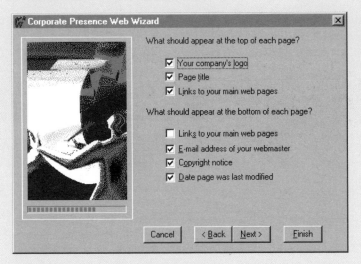

Pick a Look for Your Web Site

You also get to pick a look for your web site. Just click the Choose Web Theme button when you see it, and then choose a theme for your web site. If you like one of the themes but don't want to have a background image, you

can clear the Background Image check box. It's easy to change a web's theme later. (I describe how you do this in "Working with Themes View" on page 21.)

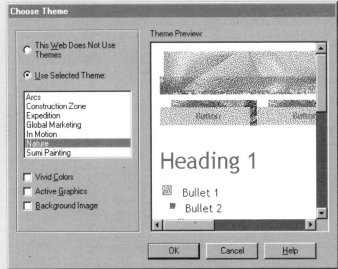

After you've picked a look for your web site, you'll be asked several additional questions and you'll be asked to provide information about the web publisher. (If the web publisher is a corporation, for example, you'll provide the corporation name and address, telephone number, and so forth.) When you finish providing these last bits of information, you're done.

The FrontPage Explorer Window

Application window

The FrontPage Explorer application window shows different views of a web site. The window shows only one web site at a time. The web site name and location appear in the application window title bar.

Views bar

The Views bar provides buttons you click to switch between different views of your web site.

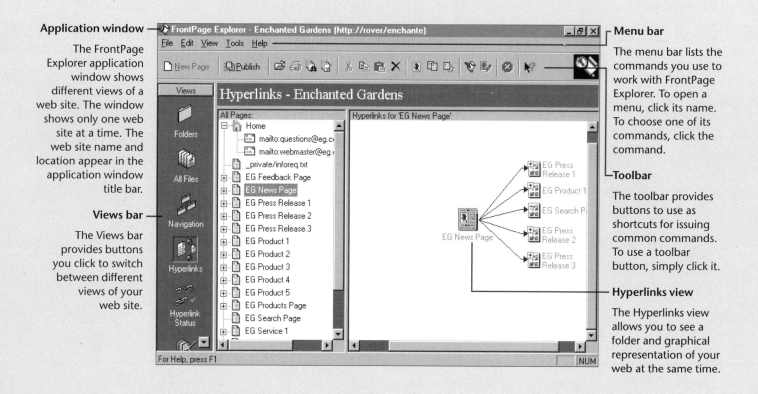

Menu bar

The menu bar lists the commands you use to work with FrontPage Explorer. To open a menu, click its name. To choose one of its commands, click the command.

Toolbar

The toolbar provides buttons to use as shortcuts for issuing common commands. To use a toolbar button, simply click it.

Hyperlinks view

The Hyperlinks view allows you to see a folder and graphical representation of your web at the same time.

Working with Folders View

Once you've created a web site, FrontPage allows you to look at and examine the web site in several different ways. The Folders view lists the web pages and images that make up your web site. Because it resembles Windows Explorer, it is easy to get used to.

TRY THIS

To change the width of a Folders view column, drag the right edge of the column heading button.

TIP

All Files view. *All Files view is similar to Folders view, except it lists the folder location of a web page or image instead of displaying it graphically. It also shows whether a web page is an orphan (not connected by hyperlinks to other pages in the web site). By default, All Files view lists web pages and images alphabetically by name, but you can sort them the same way as you do in Folders view.*

Use Folders View to List Web Pages and Images

1 Open the web site you want to view.

2 Click the Folders button on the Views bar.

3 Click a column heading button to sort the web pages.

◆ Click the Name button to sort web pages and images alphabetically by name.

◆ Click the Title button to sort web pages and images alphabetically by web page or image title.

◆ Click the Size button to sort web pages by size (from smallest to largest).

◆ Click the Type button to sort web pages and images alphabetically by type.

◆ Click the Modified Date button to sort web pages and images by date (from latest to earliest).

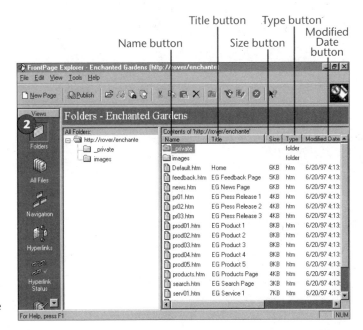

Name button · Title button · Type button · Size button · Modified Date button

Working with Hyperlinks View

You can also view your web site using Hyperlinks view. Hyperlinks view draws a map of your web showing how the web pages link together. It also displays your web site in Folders view on the left-hand side.

TRY THIS

To view your web site's images in Hyperlinks view, click the Hyperlinks To Images toolbar button. To display or hide multiple occurrences of a hyperlink on one page, click the Repeated Hyperlinks toolbar button. To display or hide bookmark hyperlinks (hyperlinks to another part of the same page), click the Hyperlinks Inside Page toolbar button.

TIP

You can change the portion of the web site displayed in Hyperlinks view by clicking a different page of the web site in Folders view.

Use Hyperlinks View to Explore Web Page Links

1 Open the web site you want to view.

2 Click the Hyperlinks button on the Views bar.

3 Click above the Hyperlinks view map background. FrontPage Explorer displays the hand icon.

4 Drag the map background to move the map. (You'll need to try this to see how it works.)

Center the Selected Web Page

1 Right-click the web page that you want to center to display the shortcut menu.

2 Choose the shortcut menu's Move To Center command. FrontPage Explorer moves the Hyperlinks view map so that the selected web page appears in the middle of the Hyperlinks view pane.

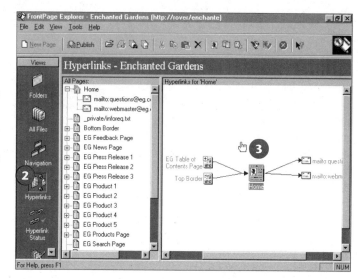

Follow a Path of Hyperlinks

1. Click the plus sign (+) on the web page or image that contains the hyperlinks you want to explore. FrontPage Explorer expands the Hyperlinks view map to show which web pages and images connect to the web page.

2. To collapse a portion of the Hyperlinks view map, click the minus sign (-) on a web page or image.

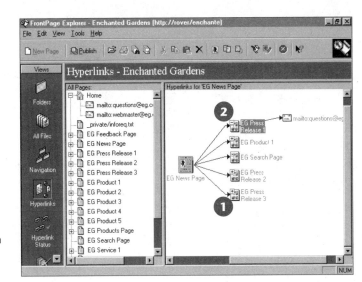

Checking Your Web Site's Hyperlinks

As you make changes to your web site (or as others make changes to it), you'll need to update, or refresh, your Hyperlinks view map regularly so that the map reflects reality. Once you've added all your web pages and inserted hyperlinks where appropriate, you'll want to check that the links work correctly. FrontPage Explorer provides two tools you can use to perform this link-checking: the Verify Hyperlinks toolbar button in the Hyperlink Status view and the Tools menu's Recalculate Hyperlinks command.

TIP

Click the Stop toolbar button to stop the verification process.

Verify Your Web Site's Hyperlinks

1. Open the web site you want to view.

2. Click the Hyperlink Status button on the Views bar.

3. Click the Verify Hyperlinks toolbar button.

4. Select an option to tell FrontPage which hyperlinks to verify.

   ◆ Click the Verify All Hyperlinks option button to verify all broken or unknown hyperlinks.

   ◆ Click the Resume Verification option button if you previously started to verify hyperlinks but stopped before completing the verification.

   ◆ Click the Verify Selected Hyperlinks option button to verify only the hyperlinks you select.

5. Click Start. When FrontPage finishes verifying the hyperlinks, it displays the status of your hyperlinks in the Hyperlink Status view window.

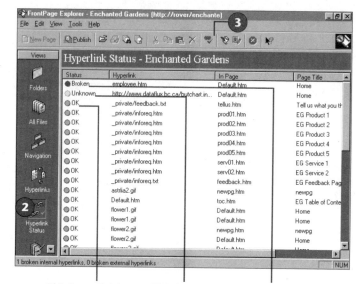

This hyperlink has been checked and found good.

This hyperlink has not been checked because it is not within the current web site.

This hyperlink has been checked and found bad.

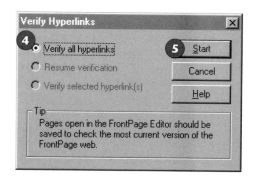

TIP

By default, Hyperlink Status view displays only broken links within the web site and unchecked links to external sources. If you want to view the status of all links, choose the View menu's Show All Hyperlinks command.

TIP

The Recalculate Hyperlinks command works in all views. It tells the web server to update your hyperlinks and remove references to deleted pages.

TIP

Replace links in selected pages only. *Click the Change In Selected Pages option button if you don't want to globally replace all occurrences of the link to the web page. Then select the page or pages you want to edit by clicking them in the list box. (Hold down the Ctrl key if you want to select multiple pages.)*

Recalculate Your Web Site's Links

1 Choose the Tools menu's Recalculate Hyperlinks command.

2 When FrontPage Explorer displays a message box that tells you link recalculation requires the efforts of your server and may take a long time, click Yes.

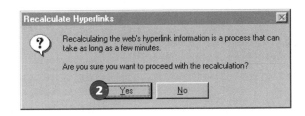

Edit Broken Links

1 Right-click any broken link in Hyperlink Status view.

2 Choose the shortcut menu's Edit Hyperlink command. FrontPage Explorer displays the Edit Hyperlink dialog box.

3 Enter the web page name in the Replace Hyperlink With text box to specify the correct link. Or click the Browse button to find the web page.

4 Click the Change In All Pages option button if you want to replace every occurrence of the link with the web page you entered in the Replace Hyperlink With text box.

5 Click Replace.

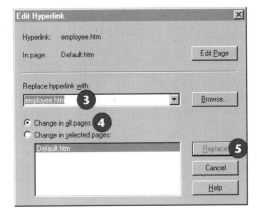

Working with Navigation View

FrontPage 98 includes a new way of viewing your web site called Navigation view. With Navigation view, you can see your web site graphically in a hierarchical format and work with it in Folders view at the same time.

TRY THIS

Click the Rotate toolbar button to rotate your navigation chart so that the pyramid branches out from left to right. Click the Size To Fit toolbar button so that you can see your entire navigation chart in the window without having to scroll back and forth with the scroll bars.

Use Navigation View to View Your Web Site Hierarchy

1 Open the web site you want to view.

2 Click the Navigation button on the Views bar.

3 Click a plus sign (+) to expand a level.

4 Click a minus sign (-) to collapse a level.

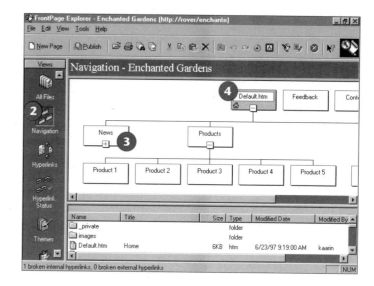

Working with Themes View

When you first created your web site, you specified whether or not you wanted to use one of FrontPage's design themes, and if so, which one. You can easily change this theme with a few quick clicks of the mouse and thereby alter the entire look of your web site.

Change Your Web Site's Theme

1 Open the web site you want to view.

2 Click the Themes button on the Views bar.

3 Click the Use Selected Theme option button.

4 Select a theme from the list box.

5 Optionally, customize the theme.

- ◆ Check the Vivid Colors box to use eye-catching colors

- ◆ Check the Active Graphics box to add dynamic bullet points and graphics to your web.

- ◆ Check the Background Image box to add or remove the defined background image.

6 Click Apply to apply the theme to your web site

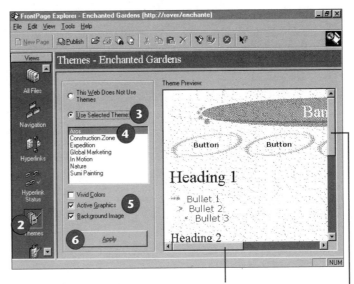

If necessary, use the scroll bars in the Theme Preview window to see all of the web page elements.

Using the To Do List

Even after you've created a framework for your web site, you still have much work to do. To help you keep track of which web pages need to be finalized and where important images need to be replaced, FrontPage Explorer includes a To Do List that you work with in Tasks view. (When you run one of the web wizards, FrontPage Explorer actually builds a preliminary To Do List for you, consisting of tasks it knows you'll need to accomplish.)

> **TIP**
>
> *FrontPage Explorer initially sorts To Do List tasks from highest priority to lowest priority.*

View and Sort the Tasks on Your To Do List

1 Click the Tasks button on the Views bar.

2 Use the scroll bars to scroll up and down or left and right in your list.

3 Click a column heading button to sort the tasks.

- ◆ Click the Status button to sort tasks by completion status.

- ◆ Click the Task button heading to sort tasks alphabetically by name.

- ◆ Click the Assigned To button to sort tasks alphabetically by the name of the person assigned to complete the task.

- ◆ Click the Priority button to sort tasks in order of decreasing priority.

- ◆ Click the Linked To button to sort tasks by the name of the web page or image to which the task relates.

- ◆ Click the Modified Date button to sort tasks by the date they were created or modified.

Status button   Assigned To button   Linked To button

Task button   Priority button   Modified Date button

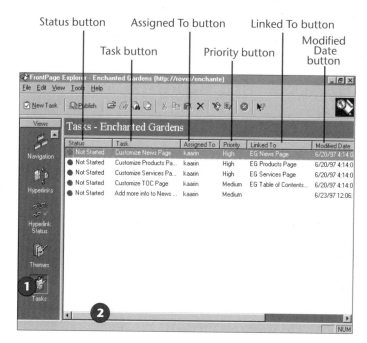

Display the To Do List History

1 Click the Tasks button on the Views bar to display the To Do List.

2 Choose the View menu's Task History command.

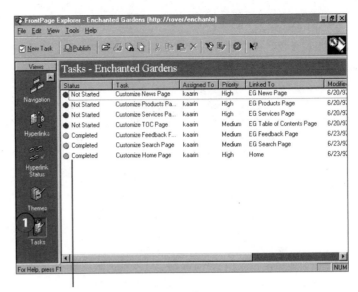

Completed tasks show up when you view the Task history.

Working with Tasks

FrontPage Explorer builds an initial list of tasks that you need to complete, which mostly consists of replacing place holders with real web content. This initial list, however, is by no means exhaustive, so you will most likely want to add new tasks to it. You might also want to view and edit descriptions of tasks currently on the list.

Add a Task to the To Do List

1 Click the Tasks button on the Views bar to display the To Do List.

2 Click the New Task toolbar button.

3 Type a name in the Task Name text box.

4 Type a person's name in the Assign To text box.

5 Select a Priority option.

6 Describe the task in the Description text box.

7 Click OK.

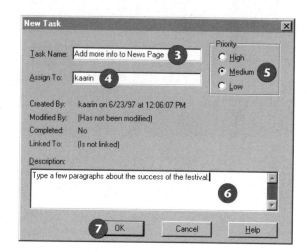

Section 3, "Working with Web Page Text," explains how FrontPage Editor works.

Edit a Task Assignment, Description, or Priority

1 Click the Tasks button on the Views bar to display the To Do List.

2 Right-click the task.

3 Choose the shortcut menu's Edit Task command.

4 Edit the task details.

◆ Assign the task to a different person by typing a new name in the Assign To text box.

◆ Change the task priority by clicking a different Priority option button.

◆ Change the task description by typing new text in the Description text box or by editing the existing text.

5 Click OK.

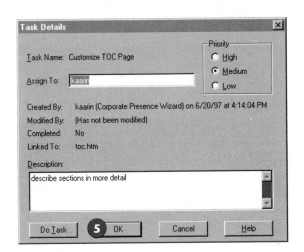

Completing Tasks

Completing the tasks on your To Do List is by far the most time-consuming part of building your web site. Completing these tasks involves filling individual web pages with graphic and textual content, which necessarily includes several critical decisions, such as what information to include, how to organize it, and how to lay it out. As you complete tasks, you'll want to mark them off your To Do List so that you can monitor your progress.

● Not Started
○ Completed

Perform a Task

1. Click the Tasks button on the Views bar to display the To Do List.

2. Right-click the task.

3. Choose the shortcut menu's Do Task command. FrontPage Explorer starts FrontPage Editor, which opens the web page you need to complete the task.

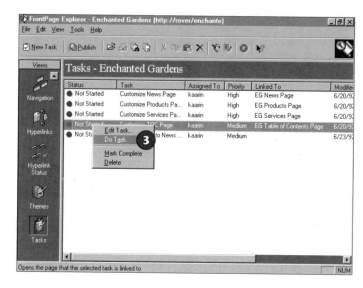

Mark a Task as Completed

1. Click the Tasks button on the Views bar to display the To Do List.

2. Right-click the task.

3. Choose the shortcut menu's Mark Complete command.

Delete a Task

1 Click the Tasks button on the Views bar to display the To Do List.

2 Right-click the task.

3 Choose the shortcut menu's Delete command.

4 When FrontPage asks you to confirm the delete, click Yes.

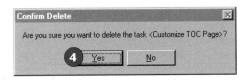

Working with Web Pages and Images

You use FrontPage Explorer not only as a way to view a web site's overall organization and layout but also as a way to open and work with specific web pages and images. In other words, you'll typically use FrontPage Explorer to start FrontPage Editor and open specific web pages. And you'll use FrontPage Explorer to start Image Composer and open specific images.

SEE ALSO

Section 3, "Working with Web Page Text," describes FrontPage Editor and how you use it to fill web pages with text.

TIP

If you are deleting a page in Navigation view, FrontPage will ask you if you want to remove the page only from the view or delete it from the entire web site. Indicate that you want to delete it from the web, and then click OK.

Open a Web Page or Image

1. Display your web site in either Folders, All Files, Navigation, or Hyperlinks view.

2. Double-click the web page or image you want to open. FrontPage Explorer starts FrontPage Editor (if you are opening a web page) or Image Composer (if you are opening an image).

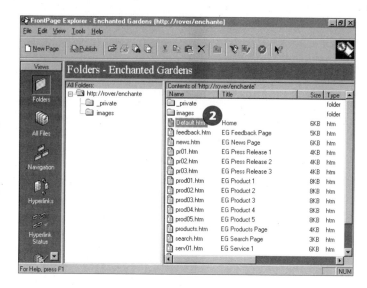

Remove a Web Page or Image from the Web Site

1. Display your web site in either Folders, All Files, Navigation, or Hyperlinks view.

2. Right-click the web page or image you want to remove from the web site.

3. Choose the shortcut menu's Delete command.

4. When FrontPage asks you to confirm the delete, click Yes.

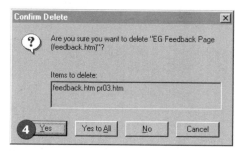

Get More Information About a Web Page or Image

1 Display your web site in either Folders, All Files, Navigation, or Hyperlinks view.

2 Right-click the web page or image you want to learn more about.

3 Choose the shortcut menu's Properties command.

4 Click the General tab, if necessary.

5 Click OK.

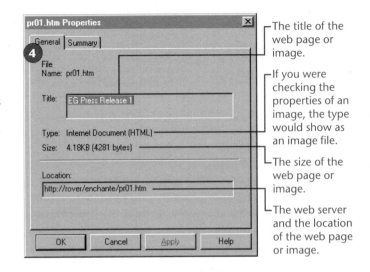

The title of the web page or image.

If you were checking the properties of an image, the type would show as an image file.

The size of the web page or image.

The web server and the location of the web page or image.

2

Importing and Exporting Web Content

If you feel more comfortable working with another program, such as a word processing or image editing program, to create web content or edit existing content, you can easily do so. Then, after you have created the content, you can import it into FrontPage to prepare for publishing on the web.

Import...
Export...

TIP

If you close all open web sites and choose the File menu's Import command, FrontPage Explorer starts the Import Web Wizard, which guides you through creating a new web from a folder.

Import a Web Page or Image

1. Open the web site where you want to place the new, imported web page or image.

2. Choose the File menu's Import command.

3. Click the Add File button.

4. Activate the Files Of Type drop-down list box; then select the type of file you want to import.

5. Use the Look In drop-down list box to find the page you want to import.

6. Select the page by double-clicking it.

7. Repeat steps 3, 4, 5, and 6 to add more web pages to the Import Web Wizard's list of pages.

8. Click OK to add the web pages and images to the open web site.

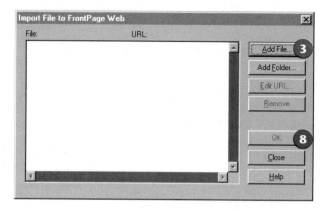

TRY THIS

To export a web page or image to a Microsoft Office application such as Microsoft Word, Microsoft Excel, or Microsoft PowerPoint, select the Microsoft Office Files entry from the Save As Type drop-down list box.

Export a Web Page or Image

1. Open the web site from which you want to export a web page or image.

2. Select the web page or image you want to export by clicking it.

3. Choose the File menu's Export command.

4. Specify the folder where you want to save the web page or image in the Save In drop-down list box.

5. Type a name in the File Name text box, if necessary.

6. Specify the format in which you want to save the web page or image using the Save As Type drop-down list box.

7. Click Save to export the web page or image.

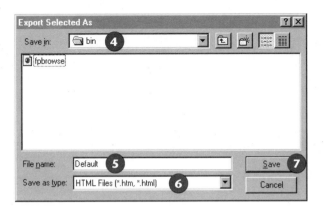

Finding and Replacing Text in a Web Site

Normally, you'll work with your web page text by using FrontPage Editor, which is described in Section 3, "Working with Web Page Text." But FrontPage Explorer also lets you work with web page text. The difference between using FrontPage Explorer and using FrontPage Editor is that FrontPage Explorer lets you work with all your web pages at the same time. For example, you can easily find and replace text strings in all of your web pages at once.

TIP

Check the Match Whole Word Only box if you want FrontPage Explorer to find only whole word occurrences of the entry in the Find What text box. Check the Match Case box if you want FrontPage Explorer to find only occurrences that exactly match the case of the entry in the Find What box.

Find Occurrences of Existing Text Fragments You Want to Edit

1 Click the Cross File Find toolbar button.

2 Type the text you want to search for in the Find What text box.

3 Select a Find In option to indicate whether you want all the web pages in the web site searched or only a specified set of web pages. (If you click the Selected Pages option button, FrontPage Explorer asks which pages you want to search.)

4 Click OK. FrontPage Explorer builds a list of web pages that contain the text.

5 To view a page immediately, double-click it. FrontPage Explorer opens FrontPage Editor; you use it to view the page and make changes.

6 To postpone viewing a page, select the page and then click the Add Task button. FrontPage Explorer adds the task to your To Do List.

7 Click Close when you are finished.

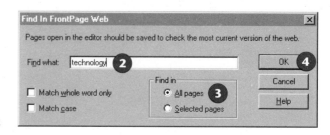

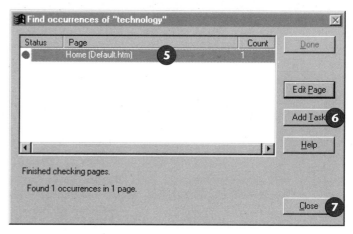

Match whole words only. *If you want to replace only whole-word occurrences of the text fragment you're searching for, check the Match Whole Word Only box. For example, if you want to replace the word* yard *with the word* lawn, *you don't want FrontPage Explorer to change the word* hal*yard to* hal*lawn.*

Replace Multiple Occurrences of Existing Text Fragments

1 Choose the Tools menu's Replace command.

2 Type the text you want to replace in the Find What text box.

3 Type the new text you want to use in the Replace With text box.

4 Select a Find In option to indicate whether you want all the web pages in the web site searched or only a specified set of web pages. (If you click the Selected Pages option button, FrontPage Explorer asks which pages you want to search.)

5 Click OK. FrontPage Explorer builds a list of web pages with the text.

6 To view a page immediately, double-click it.

7 To postpone viewing a page, select the page and then click the Add Task button. FrontPage Explorer adds the task to your To Do List.

8 Click Close when you are finished.

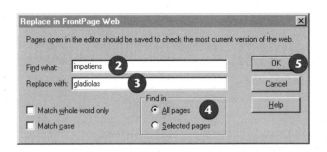

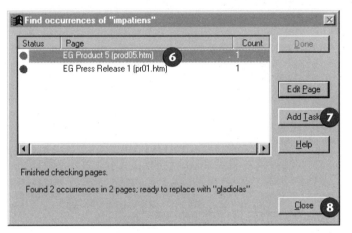

Checking Spelling in a Web Site

Just as you can use FrontPage Explorer to find and replace text across an entire web site, you can also use FrontPage Explorer to check spelling in several or all of your web pages at once.

Spell-Check Your Web Site's Pages

1 Click the Cross File Spelling toolbar button.

2 Click the All Pages option button to check the spelling of all your web pages.

3 Click Start.

4 To fix a page immediately, double-click it. FrontPage Explorer opens FrontPage Editor; you use it to make your corrections.

5 To postpone fixing a page's misspellings, select the page and then click the Add Task button. FrontPage Explorer adds this task to your To Do List.

6 Click Close when you are finished.

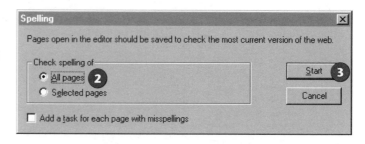

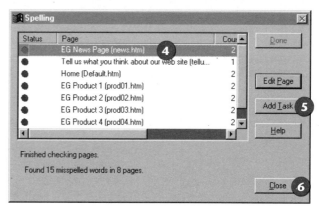

Working with Web Page Text

Once you've created a new web site—remember this is a basic framework of blank web pages ready to fill with content—you can begin creating web page documents. To do this, you fill your web pages with text, images, and other information.

In this section, you learn how to fill your pages with textual content—words and numbers—by using Microsoft FrontPage Editor. FrontPage Editor works very much like a word processing program. So if you've used a word processing program before, particularly Microsoft Word, you'll find FrontPage Editor easy to learn and use.

In later sections, you'll learn how to fill your pages with other types of content. Section 4 describes how to work with images, for example. Section 8 describes how you can use special effects, such as sound and video clips, in your web pages.

Where Do I Get the Text?

Good question. Books such as this often skip over the creation of your content, especially the creation of your textual content. They tend to assume that you have all this great information—neatly organized and highly polished, of course—that's just waiting to be dropped into a fancy set of web pages.

For purposes of this section, I have to pretend that you have all this content ready to drop into a set of web pages, too. But, actually, before you start any real work on a web site's pages, you need your content.

Content Development: The Big Picture

I can't really tell you how you create the specific textual information you need. I don't know whether you're trying to web-publish corporate marketing literature, a scary true-crime novel, or information about a worthy nonprofit organization you volunteer for. Nevertheless, I want to remind you that the very first thing you need to do when you begin a web publishing project is to develop your content. If you don't already have your content—and particularly your textual content—you may be putting the cart before the horse.

This information gathering and organizing is actually the hardest part of publishing something on an external or internal web. I mention this here because my experience is that most people ignore the content in their rush to jump onto this particular technology bandwagon. So let me throw out some rules of thumb.

Allow at least a couple of days to create any substantial, information-rich web page that's of, say, magazine-article or magazine-column length. Then you will need another day or two to copy-edit and fact-check one article (just to make sure you don't commit embarrassing grammatical errors or appear uninformed because of a factual mistake). If everything functions like clockwork, that totals about a week of time per web article. For a small web site with a dozen articles, you're probably looking at three months of work.

If you want to publish the equivalent of a 500-page book using an internal or external web, your efforts probably quadruple. In this case, maybe you've got six months of research and writing and another six months of editing. All totaled, then, you're looking at maybe a year of effort.

If you're planning a more substantial web publishing presence or project, the numbers quickly grow even larger. The point I want to emphasize is this: content—the very essence of any good web site—is expensive and time-consuming to produce.

Conventional wisdom says you need to update your web site's content continually if you're going to get people to revisit your web site. Assuming you accept the conventional wisdom—and I think you probably should—that means you need to develop new content on a regular basis to keep bringing people back to the web site for repeat visits. (An exception to this rule about needing to develop new content is when people will use your web site for reference—for example, an online employee manual, product pricing or technical specifications information, and downloadable files [such as for IRS tax forms or Microsoft Windows utilities].)

I don't want to discourage you from publishing web pages on the Internet or an intranet. The technology is here to stay, and it opens up wonderful opportunities for sharing information. I just want you to know that, as crazy as it sounds, web publishing is probably much more like the print publishing or television industries than most people realize. It's the content that really matters— not the method used to deliver the information.

A Content Development Loophole

In fairness, I should alert you to the possibility—nay, the probability—that you actually do have significant volumes of raw content already developed. Or at least halfway developed. Presumably you or your organization have lots of textual information that's already collected and organized. Product literature. Employee manuals and directories. Perhaps annual reports or newsletters. You know the sort of stuff I'm talking about. You need to look closely at this material to determine its suitability. But it's

quite likely that some of this material—the information that customers and employees most often ask for—is suitable for a web site.

Content Development: The Little Picture

If you have little bits of information from here and there that you want to work into your web pages, you can type that content directly in the web page. (I'll talk about this in a minute.) But you want the bulk of your content available in electronic files. That means you want the great majority of your text available as text files or word processing documents. (The word processing documents produced by most word processing programs will work just fine.)

You also want any other content you'll include in your web pages available in electronic, or digital, form. This means that you'll need to either scan any artwork or photographs you want to use or re-create this artwork using a graphics or drawing program. (This section describes how you enter textual content in your web pages. The next section describes how you enter images in your web pages.)

Entering Text in a Page

Once you've created a web site, you're ready to begin filling your pages with text. If you've ever worked with Microsoft Word, you'll find that this process works very much like you would expect. For the most part, you click a location within a web page document to position the cursor, and then you begin typing.

> **TIP**
>
> *If you make a mistake entering text, use the Backspace key to erase your entry. Then begin typing again.*

> **TIP**
>
> *If you enter a string of text that FrontPage recognizes as a URL, it will convert the text into a hyperlink to that location. For more information about hyperlinks, see pages 88–89.*

Open the Web Page

1. Start FrontPage, and open the web site in FrontPage Explorer.

2. Double-click the web page you want to open. This starts FrontPage Editor and opens the selected web page.

Name	Title
astrlia2.gif	astrlia2.gif
bicycle2.gif	bicycle2.gif
Default.htm ②	Home
example.htm	Example Frameset
feedback.htm	EG Feedback Page
feedback.txt	_private/feedback.txt

Enter New Text

1. Click to place the insertion point where you want to add new text.

2. Type the new text in the web page.

3. Press the Enter key to end one paragraph of text and begin another paragraph.

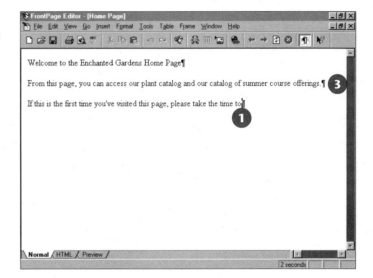

Delete Existing Text

1 Select the text you want to delete by clicking the first character you want to delete and dragging the mouse to the last character you want to delete.

2 Press the Delete key.

Our Mission¶

We want to create products **and services** that deliver extraordinary benefits to our customers, the distribution channel, and our readers. ¶

Our Mission¶

We want to create products that deliver extraordinary benefits our customers, the distribution channel, and our readers. ¶

Undo Erroneous Text Entry and Editing

1 If you want to reverse the effect of your last text entry or editing action, choose the Edit menu's Undo command. Or click the Undo toolbar button.

Replace a Single Occurrence of Existing Text

1 Select the text you want to edit, or change, by clicking the first character you want to replace and then dragging the mouse to the last character you want to replace.

2 Type the text you want to replace the selected text.

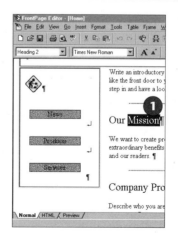

3

Finding and Replacing Text

If you have a recurring word or string of text that you want to find or replace in a web page, you can use the Edit menu's Find and Replace commands to save yourself the time and trouble of reading an entire web page document and manually replacing each occurrence of the text. Using these commands also lowers your chances of missing occurrences of the text string or of introducing new typographical errors to the web page.

SEE ALSO

For information on how to find and replace text across all pages of a web site, see pages 32–33.

TIP

Check the Match Case box if you want FrontPage Editor to find only the text in the document that matches the case of the text entered in the Find text box.

Find Occurrences of Existing Text Fragments

1 Choose the Edit menu's Find command.

2 Type the text you want to find in the Find What text box.

3 Check the Match Whole Word Only box, if appropriate.

4 Check the Match Case box, if appropriate.

5 Optionally, click a Direction option button to specify whether FrontPage Editor should look from the insertion point forward to the end of the document or from the insertion point backward to the beginning of the document.

6 Click Find Next to find the next occurrence of the text entered in the Find What text box.

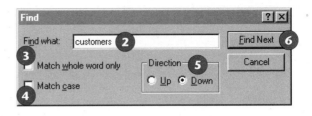

Check the Match Whole Word Only box if you want FrontPage Editor to replace only whole word occurrences of the text fragment you're searching for. For example, if you want to replace the word war *with the word* battle, *you don't want FrontPage Editor changing the word* hardware *to* hardbattlee.

Replace Multiple Occurrences of Existing Text Fragments

1 Choose the Edit menu's Replace command.

2 Type the text you want to replace in the Find What text box.

3 Type the new text you want to use in the Replace With text box.

4 Click Find Next to find the next occurrence of the text entered in the Find What text box.

5 Click Replace to replace the selected occurrence of the text entered in the Find What text box with the text entered in the Replace With text box.

6 Click Replace All to replace every occurrence of the text entered in the Find What text box with the text entered in the Replace With text box.

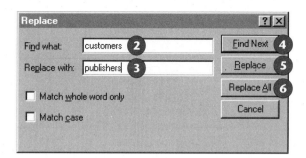

Inserting Text Objects

At times you may want to insert a text object in a web page rather than entering the text using FrontPage Editor. For example, if you already have a document that you created in a word processing program, you might want to insert it in a web page instead of retyping it. Or you might need to add a symbol or character not on your keyboard (especially if you are creating a multilanguage site).

Open

TIP

Save documents as RTF files. *When you're creating a word processing document that you plan to use in FrontPage Editor, tell your word processor to save the document as a Rich Text Format, or RTF, file. You probably do this by using the word processor's File menu's Save As command.*

Insert a Text File

1 Click to place the insertion point where you want to add new text.

2 Choose the Insert menu's File command.

3 Specify the location of the file you want to insert in the Look In drop-down list box.

4 Specify the format of the file you want to insert in the Files Of Type drop-down list box.

5 When FrontPage Editor displays the file in the list box, double-click the file to insert its contents in the web page at the insertion point location.

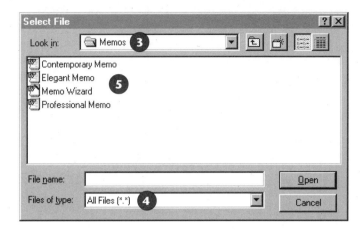

Double-click a character in the Symbol box to insert it.

Insert a Symbol

1 Click in your web page to place the insertion point where you want to insert the new symbol.

2 Choose the Insert menu's Symbol command.

3 Click the symbol you want to insert. You can insert more than one symbol at a time by clicking additional symbols.

4 Click the Insert button to place the selected symbol at the insertion point location.

5 Click the Close button to close the Symbol dialog box.

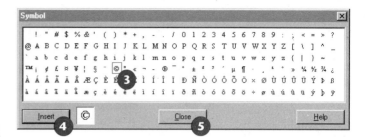

Polishing Your Web Page Prose

FrontPage comes with the Microsoft Office Spelling and Thesaurus tools. Once you've entered all your text and made your editing changes, use the spelling tool to find and correct any spelling errors. You may also want to use the Thesaurus tool to, well, improve the quality of your prose.

TIP

To check the spelling in only a portion of the web page, simply select the text you want to spell-check before choosing the Tools menu's Spelling command.

SEE ALSO

See page 34 for information on how to spell-check across the entire web site.

Spell-Check Your Web Page

1 Choose the Tools menu's Spelling command. If FrontPage Editor finds a misspelling, it displays the Spelling dialog box.

2 If FrontPage Editor shows the correct spelling in the Suggestions list box, click the word.

3 If nothing appears in the Suggestions list box and you know the correct spelling, type it in the Change To text box.

4 Click the Change button to correct only this occurrence of the misspelling. Click the Change All button to correct this occurrence and every other occurrence of the misspelling.

5 If the word that FrontPage Editor thinks is misspelled isn't really misspelled, click the Ignore button to ignore only this occurrence of the word. Click the Ignore All button to ignore this and every other occurrence of the word.

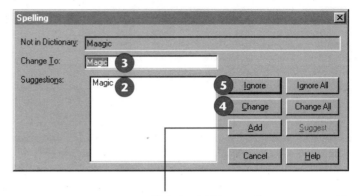

Click the Add button if you want to add the word to FrontPage's dictionary.

Use the Thesaurus

1 Select the word you want to replace with a different word.

2 Choose the Tools menu's Thesaurus command.

3 Verify the Meanings list box shows the correct word definition.

4 Select a word from the Replace With Synonym list box. FrontPage Editor places the selected replacement word in the Replace With Synonym text box.

5 Click Replace.

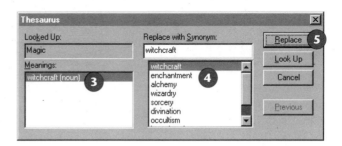

3

Moving and Copying Text

FrontPage Editor lets you perform the same cut, copy, and paste operations as does your word processor. This ability to cut, copy, and paste makes it easy to move and copy text within and between web page documents.

Move Text Within a Web Page

1 Select the text you want to move.

2 Click the text selection, and then drag it to the new location.

Move Text Between Web Pages

1 Choose the File menu's Open command, and then double-click the web page with the text you want to move.

2 Choose the File menu's Open command, and then double-click the web page in which you want to place the text.

3 Choose the Window menu's Tile command. FrontPage Editor displays windows for both web pages within the FrontPage Editor application window.

4 Select the text you want to move from the first web page window.

5 Click the text selection, and then drag the text to the new location in the second web page window.

Our Mission

We want to improve people's lives by simplifying the complexity of technology

Enchanted Gardens Productions: **1**

Enchanted Gardens Productions: Our Mission **2**

We want to improve people's lives by simplifying the complexity of technology

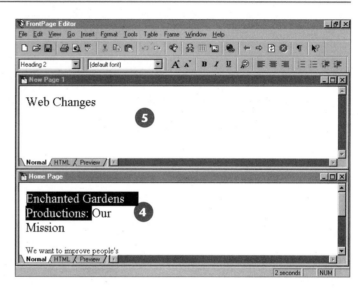

Copy Text Within a Web Page

1 Select the text you want to copy.

2 Click the text selection, hold down the Ctrl key, and then drag the text to the new location.

Copy Text Between Web Pages

1 Choose the File menu's Open command, and then double-click the web page with the text you want to copy.

2 Choose the File menu's Open command, and then double-click the web page in which you want to place a copy of the text.

3 Choose the Window menu's Tile command. FrontPage Editor displays windows for both web pages within the FrontPage Editor application window.

4 Select the text you want to copy from the first web page window.

5 Click the text selection, hold down the Ctrl key, and then drag the text to the new location in the second web page window.

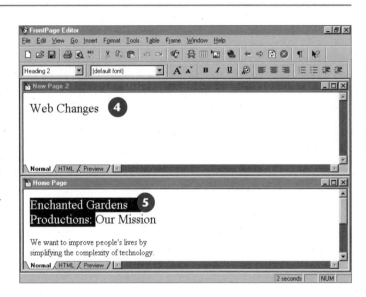

Formatting Characters

Once you've entered and polished your web page text, you can then add character-level formatting, such as boldfacing, italics, and underlining. You can also color text and change the font. This character-level formatting makes your web page more legible and more interesting.

EnchantED

Add Text Effects

1 Select the text you want to format.

2 Click one of the following toolbar buttons.

- ◆ Bold

- ◆ Italic

- ◆ Underline

Color Text

1 Select the text you want to recolor.

2 Click the Text Color toolbar button.

3 Click the square that displays the color you want to use for the selected text.

4 Click OK.

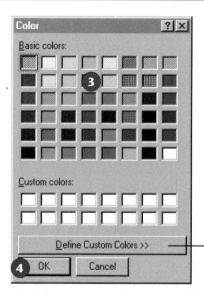

Click the Define Custom Colors button to create a custom color.

Specify the Font

1 Select the text for which you want to specify a font.

2 Activate the Change Font drop-down list box on the Formatting toolbar.

3 Select the font you want to use for the selected text.

Key Benefits

- Great exercise
- Reduces stress
- Fun for the whole family

Creating Headings and Subheadings

To create headings and subheadings within a web page, you use FrontPage Editor's built-in heading styles: heading 1—the highest-level heading—heading 2, heading 3, and so on through heading 6—the lowest-level heading.

TRY THIS

You can also create or edit headings by selecting the heading text and using the Change Style drop-down list box on the Format toolbar to specify the heading style.

Create a Heading

1 Type the text you want to use as a heading, and then press the Enter key.

2 Right-click the heading text.

3 Choose the shortcut menu's Paragraph Properties command.

4 Select a heading style from the list box.

5 Click OK, and FrontPage Editor turns the selected text into a heading.

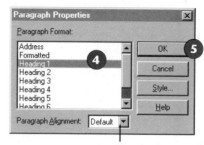

Use the Paragraph Alignment drop-down list box to specify the paragraph alignment.

Create a Subheading

1 Type the text you want to use as a subheading, and then press the Enter key.

2 Right-click the subheading text.

3 Choose the shortcut menu's Paragraph Properties command.

4 Select a heading style from the list box.

5 Click OK, and FrontPage Editor turns the selected text into a subheading.

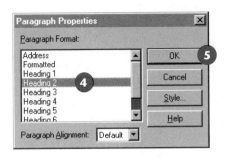

3

Formatting Paragraphs

FrontPage Editor supports several varieties of paragraph-level formatting—indenting paragraphs, aligning paragraphs horizontally across the page, and even breaking lines within paragraphs. You create paragraphs by entering a block of text and then pressing the Enter key. Pressing the Enter key signals FrontPage Editor that the text should be considered a paragraph.

> **TIP**
>
> *You might want to break a line of text without creating a new paragraph to prevent the last line of a paragraph from having a single word in it.*

> **TIP**
>
> *To display or hide format marks (the nonprinting page elements such as paragraph marks), click the Show/Hide Formats toolbar button.*

Break a Line of Text Without Creating a New Paragraph

1 Click to place the insertion point where you want to break a line without creating a new paragraph.

2 Hold down the Shift key while pressing Enter, and FrontPage Editor breaks the line but doesn't create a new paragraph.

Change Paragraph Alignment

1 Select the paragraph you want to align across the page.

2 Click one of the following toolbar buttons.

- ◆ Align Left, to align the paragraph against the left edge of the page

- ◆ Center, to center the paragraph horizontally

- ◆ Align Right, to align the paragraph against the right edge of the page

Our Mission:¶

We want to improve people's lives by simplifying the complexity of technology. ⌐

We want to provide high-quality products and services by creating teams of high-quality people. We want to create products and provide services that deliver extraordinary benefits to our customers, the distribution channel, and our readers.¶

This nonprinting character is a line break.

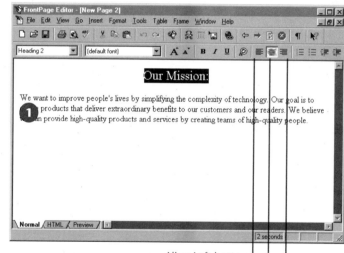

Align Left button
Center button
Align Right button

Change Paragraph Indentation

1 Select the paragraph you want to indent or unindent.

2 Click one of the following toolbar buttons.

◆ Increase Indent, to indent the paragraph

◆ Decrease Indent, to unindent the paragraph

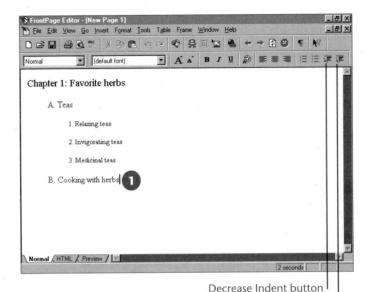

Decrease Indent button
Increase Indent button

3

Adding Horizontal Lines

Web pages often employ horizontal lines to visually separate a web page into sections. Horizontal lines are not only aesthetically pleasing but they also make long documents easier to read. You can think of horizontal lines as the World Wide Web equivalent to the page breaks that you would add to a word processing document to define what information should print on each piece of paper.

Insert a Horizontal Line Between Two Paragraphs

1. Place the insertion point at the beginning of the paragraph in front of which you want to insert a line.

2. Choose the Insert menu's Horizontal Line command.

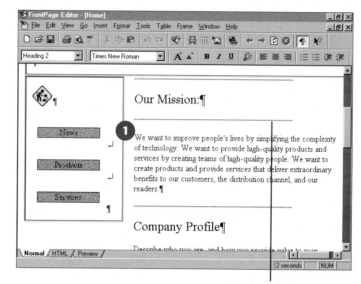

Horizontal line

TIP

If the width of the line is set to 100 percent of the window, then the alignment setting has no effect.

TIP

If you apply a theme to a web page, only the alignment of a horizontal line can be changed.

Customize a Horizontal Line

1 Right-click the horizontal line you want to customize.

2 Choose the shortcut menu's Horizontal Line Properties command.

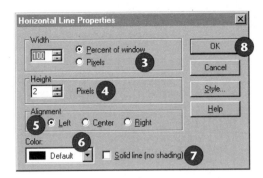

3 Specify the width of the line (how long it should be) by using the Width box and option buttons.

4 Specify the height of the line (how thick it should be) in the Height box.

5 Specify the position of the line (whether it's left-aligned, centered, or right-aligned) by using the Alignment option buttons.

6 Select a color for the line from the Color drop-down list box.

7 Check the Solid Line (No Shading) box if you don't want FrontPage Editor to draw a shadow for the line.

8 Click OK.

Working with Paragraph Lists

You can rearrange a set of paragraphs—remember, a paragraph is just a block of text that ends where you've pressed the Enter key—so that they appear as a numbered list, a bulleted list, or some other specially formatted list.

Company Profile

※ Fun
※ Fast
※ Furious

TIP

To remove the numbering from a set of paragraphs you've turned into a numbered list, select the numbered list and then click the Numbered List toolbar button again.

Create a Numbered List

1 Select the paragraphs you want to convert to a numbered list.

2 Click the Numbered List toolbar button.

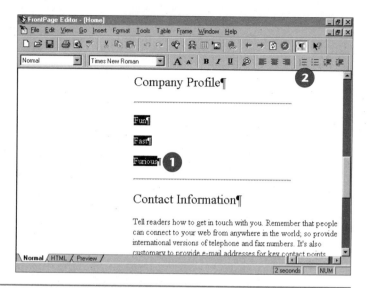

Customize a Numbered List

1 Select the numbered list or the set of paragraphs you want to convert to a numbered list.

2 Choose the Format menu's Bullets And Numbering command.

3 Click the Numbers tab.

4 Click the picture you want your numbered list to look like.

5 Optionally, indicate which number FrontPage Editor should use for the first item in the numbered list.

6 Click OK.

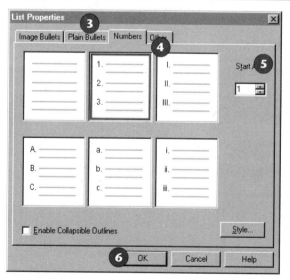

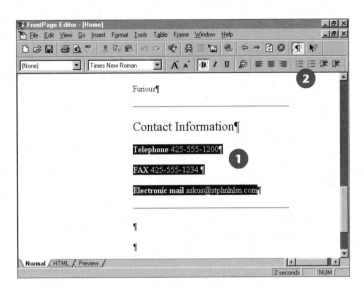

Create a Bulleted List

1 Select the paragraphs you want to convert to a bulleted list.

2 Click the Bulleted List toolbar button.

Customize a Bulleted List

1 Select the bulleted list or the set of paragraphs you want to convert to a bulleted list.

2 Choose the Format menu's Bullets And Numbering command.

3 Click the Image Bullets or Plain Bullets tab.

4 Click the picture you want your bulleted list to look like.

5 Click OK.

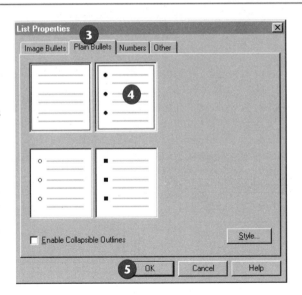

Working with Web Page Images

After you've created your web pages and filled them with text—activities described in earlier sections of this book—you're ready to liven up your pages with images. Microsoft FrontPage makes this portion of your web publishing work easy. You'll find that placing images in a web page is much the same as placing images in Microsoft Word documents or Microsoft Excel workbooks. Before you begin placing images in your web pages, however, take a moment to consider what you want to accomplish with your images and how you want to go about your work.

Inserting Images

If you've ever worked with Microsoft Word and have inserted an image, you'll find the process works much the same way in FrontPage. In most instances, you click a location within your web page document to position the cursor, and then you insert the image by clicking the Insert Image toolbar button.

TIP

Click the File button if you want to insert an image file from another location on your computer. Click the World Wide Web button to locate an image on the World Wide Web.

TIP

FrontPage recognizes the following image file types: GIF, JPG, BMP, EPS, PCX, RAS, TGA, TIF, and WMF.

Insert an Image

1 Click to place the insertion point where you want to add your image.

2 Click the Insert Image toolbar button.

3 Select an image file from the list box, or specify an image on the World Wide Web by typing the image's URL in the URL text box.

4 Click OK to insert the image.

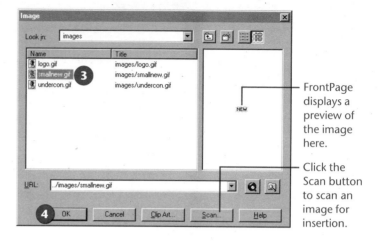

FrontPage displays a preview of the image here.

Click the Scan button to scan an image for insertion.

The Microsoft FrontPage 98 Bonus Pack includes Microsoft Image Composer, an image editing program that you can use to create and edit images. Just click the Show Image Editor toolbar button in FrontPage Explorer to start the program.

If you insert an image that is not in the GIF or JPEG format, FrontPage converts it to GIF format if it has 256 or fewer colors or to JPEG format if it has more than 256 colors.

You can also insert an image from another application by opening the image in the other application, copying it to the Clipboard, and then pasting it into a web page using the Paste toolbar button in FrontPage Editor.

Insert an Image from Clip Art

1 Click to place the insertion point where you want to add your image.

2 Click the Insert Image toolbar button.

3 Click the Clip Art button.

4 Select a clip art category from the Category list box.

5 Select the image you want to insert.

6 Click Insert.

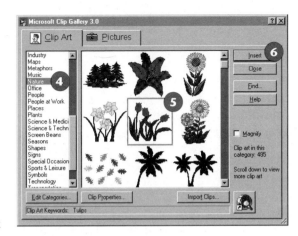

Using Images Wisely

Images, whether photographs or simple illustrations, can be used to add zest to your web site, illustrate a point, or simply make it more fun for people to visit your site. The challenge is to use images wisely while taking into account the opportunities and the limitations they introduce.

Let's start with the most frustrating issue first: the problem of lengthy transmission times. Unfortunately, images take time—sometimes a long time—to load. It's not uncommon for the graphic content of a web page to equal 90 percent of its total size. A 50-kilobyte web page, for example, might contain 5 kilobytes of text and 45 kilobytes of imagery. What that means, of course, is that the graphic content is responsible for 90 percent of the transmission time when a viewer loads a web page. Perhaps that's satisfactory when the imagery represents an important part of the web page content. But those percentages are difficult to defend when the imagery is merely gratuitous. (Note that a 50-kilobyte page takes about 14 seconds to download using a standard 28.8-kilobit-per-second modem.) As you add images to your web pages, therefore, you'll want to do so judiciously. And you'll need to monitor the sizes of the images you add (keeping in mind the time it takes to download images using a 28.8-Kbps modem) so that you don't overburden your visitors with unnecessarily large web pages.

Transmission times represent only one of the challenges of using images wisely, however. Another major challenge you'll encounter is simply making good graphic designs. Although people are quick to add images to web pages (just because they can), producing attractive, highly graphical web pages is more difficult than most design novices realize. For example, you need to balance the imagery you use for a page so that it doesn't look lopsided or weirdly asymmetrical. You need to work with sets of images that are compatible both within a page and across a web site. And, of course, you need to create color schemes that are eye-pleasing.

Recognize, too, that people visiting your site may use different size monitors, a variety of display resolutions, and even textual rather than graphical web browsers. So make sure you consider the full range of visitors who will browse your web site. Check out your site on as many different types of computers as possible. This will give you a feel for how other people are actually seeing your site.

Images created for print publications typically require editing to look good in digital form. Printers use much higher resolutions than do computer screens. Therefore, even though the text content of your printed brochures or annual reports converts easily to a web page, and even though FrontPage expertly converts images to the graphic file formats used in web publishing (GIF and JPEG), you may still need to clean up and resize images if they are to work well on screen and for your web site.

Furthermore, multimedia components such as images occupy a lot of space on the web server, so if you have server space limitations, you'll need to keep this in mind as you add images to your web pages. It's a good idea to delete any images you're no longer using from the web site by right-clicking them in FrontPage Explorer and choosing the shortcut menu's Delete command.

Cropping and Resizing Images

If you need to crop or resize your images, it is always best to do so in an image editing program such as Image Composer so that they do not lose quality or become distorted. Nonetheless, you might have to edit your images slightly in FrontPage Editor as well so that they fit around the text just right.

Crop an Image

1 Select the image by clicking it.

2 Click the Crop button on the Image toolbar.

3 Drag the cropping handles inward to crop the image to the portion you want.

4 Press the Enter key.

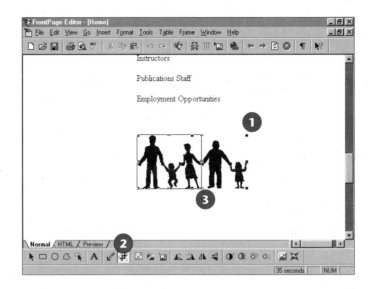

Resize an Image

1 Select the image by clicking it.

2 Drag a corner selection handle outward to increase the image's size. Or drag a corner selection handle inward to decrease an image's size.

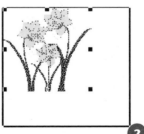

After you select an image, FrontPage Editor adds selection handles to the image.

4

Copying and Moving Images on a Web Page

After you've placed an image on your web page, you may find that the image doesn't look the way you had expected it would. Luckily, with FrontPage Editor, you can easily move the image around on the page, or you can copy and paste the image so that it does not stand alone on the page.

TIP

If you make a mistake and insert the copy of the image in the wrong location, click the Undo toolbar button to undo the paste.

Copy an Image

1. Select the image by clicking it.
2. Click the Copy toolbar button.
3. Click to place the insertion point where you want to add the copy of the image.
4. Click the Paste toolbar button.

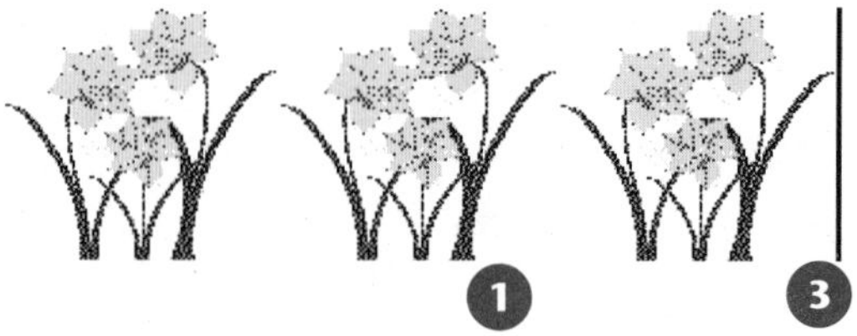

Move an Image

1. Select the image by clicking it.
2. Click the Cut toolbar button.
3. Click to place the insertion point where you want to move the image.
4. Click the Paste toolbar button.

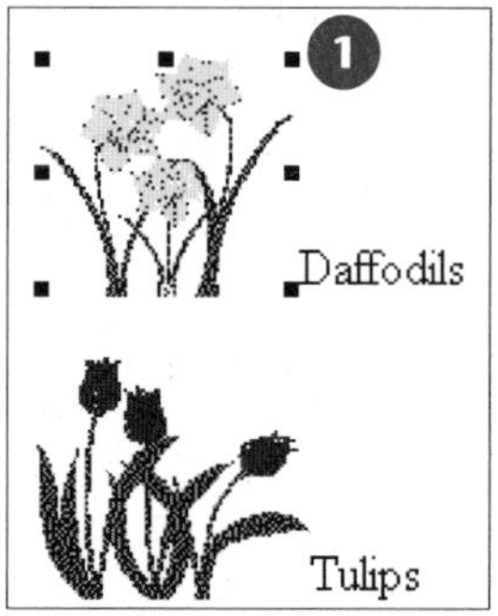

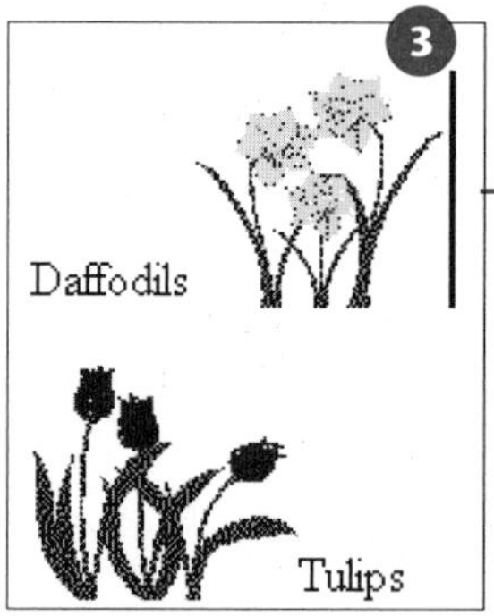

Here's how the web page fragment looks after moving the image.

Move or Copy an Image with the Mouse

1 Select the image by clicking it.

2 Drag the selected image to its new location. If you want to make a copy of the image, hold down the Ctrl key while you drag it. If you don't want to make a copy and just want to move the image, don't hold down the Ctrl key.

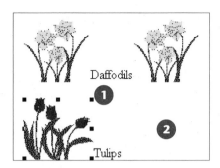

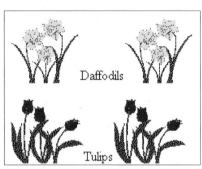

4

Copying and Moving Images to Other Locations

Once you have an image edited so that it is just the way you want it, you can then copy it or move it to a web page. By doing so, you can easily duplicate the overall effect of another web page in the current web site, or you can import a special effect created by another program.

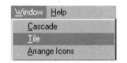

TRY THIS

You can also copy images between pages by using the mouse. To do this, select the image by clicking it, hold down the Ctrl key, and then drag the image to a new location.

Copy an Image Between Web Pages

1 Open the web page with the image you want to duplicate and the web page in which you want to place the copy of the image.

2 Choose the Window menu's Tile command.

3 Select the image you want to copy from the first web page by clicking it.

4 Click the Copy toolbar button.

5 Click to place the insertion point in the second web page where you want to add the copy of the image.

6 Click the Paste toolbar button.

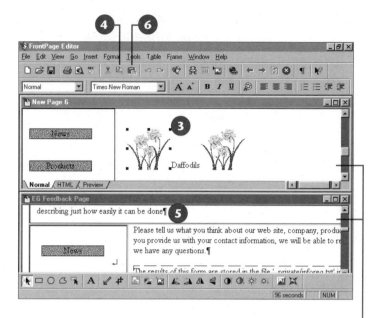

After you choose the Window menu's Tile command, both web pages are visible in the FrontPage Editor application window.

Copy an Image Between Other Types of Documents

1 Right-click the Windows Taskbar.

2 Choose the shortcut menu's Tile Vertically command.

3 Click to select the image from the other application.

4 Hold down the mouse button as you drag the image to the FrontPage Editor window.

5 Release the mouse button.

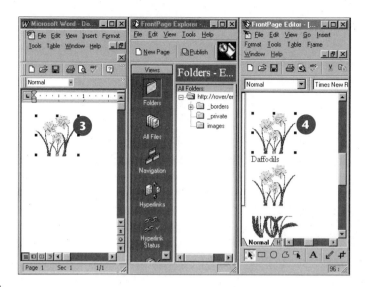

Adding Special Effects to Images

You can change the properties of any element in a web page, including the properties of an image. For example, some images might look better transparent, precisely aligned on the page, or with a border.

TRY THIS

You can increase or decrease an image's contrast and brightness by using the Contrast and Brightness buttons on the Image toolbar.

Make an Image Transparent

1 Select the image by clicking it.

2 Click the Make Transparent button on the Image toolbar.

3 Click a color of the image that you want to make transparent.

Align the Image on the Page

1 Right-click the image you want to edit.

2 Choose the shortcut menu's Image Properties command.

3 Click the Appearance tab.

4 Select the alignment option of your choice from the Alignment drop-down list box.

5 Click OK.

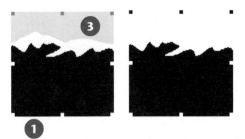

Here's how the image looks after a portion of the image has been made transparent.

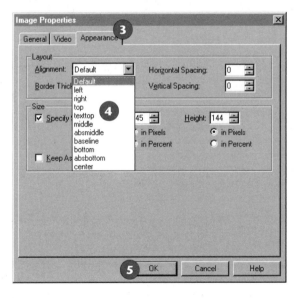

Add a Border to an Image

1 Right-click the image you want to edit.

2 Choose the shortcut menu's Image Properties command.

3 Click the Appearance tab.

4 Enter a value greater than zero in the Border Thickness box.

5 Click OK.

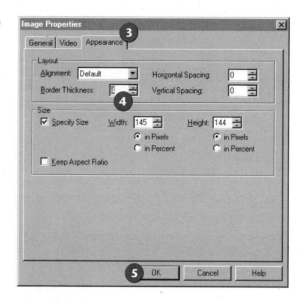

Here's how the image looks after a border has been added.

Changing Image File Format

Depending on the source and content of your image, you might want to change its file format. The file format and format properties of an image effect the image's quality and its size. GIF and JPEG formats are the most popular image formats for use on the web because they are smaller in size than other image formats and therefore take less time to transmit.

Convert an Image to JPEG Format

1 Right-click the image you want to edit.

2 Choose the shortcut menu's Image Properties command.

3 Click the General tab.

4 Click the JPEG option button.

5 Select the image quality by adjusting the up and down arrows in the Quality box.

6 Click OK.

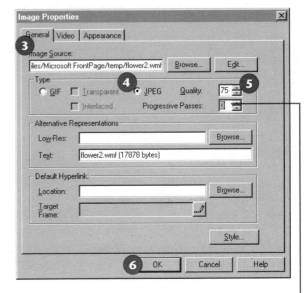

If you enter a value larger than zero in the Progressive Passes box, the image will be displayed gradually in layers, each with increasing detail and definition.

Convert an Image to GIF Format

1 Right-click the image you want to edit.

2 Choose the shortcut menu's Image Properties command.

3 Click the General tab.

4 Click the GIF option button.

5 Click OK.

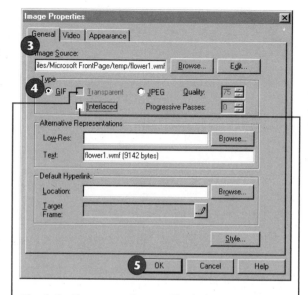

Check the Transparent box to make the GIF image transparent, if appropriate.

Check the Interlaced box to make the GIF image interlaced, if appropriate.

4

Changing the Way Images Are Displayed

As you create your web site, you need to keep in mind the numerous different ways in which your potential web site visitors browse the web. Some people choose to browse only text so that they can dramatically reduce the time it takes to load web pages. Other people have access to only older versions of browsers or to slow connections. The art in creating a web site involves accommodating these various forms of web browsing. Creating a text-only or low-resolution representation of your image allows all visitors to get a glimpse of what the image represents and peruse your web pages with ease.

Create a Text-Only Representation of an Image

1 Right-click the image you want to edit.

2 Choose the shortcut menu's Image Properties command.

3 Click the General tab.

4 Type a label that describes the image.

5 Click OK.

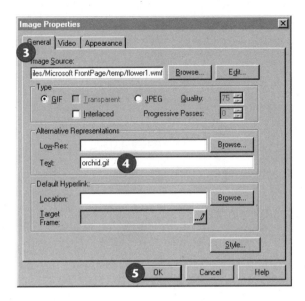

Create a Low-Resolution Substitution of an Image

1 Right-click the image you want to edit.

2 Choose the shortcut menu's Image Properties command.

3 Click the General tab.

4 Click the Browse button in the Alternative Representations box.

5 Use the Select Alternate Image dialog box to locate a low-resolution image you've created.

6 Double-click the image you want to use as an alternate.

7 Click OK.

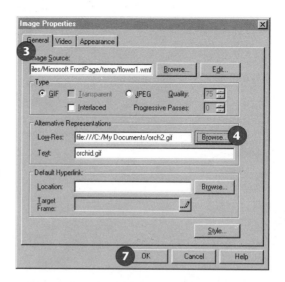

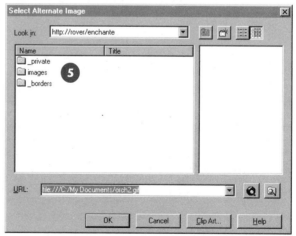

Adding Hyperlinks to Images

Images can do more than just spruce up a page. They can also have hyperlinks attached to them. When a visitor clicks on the image, he or she will be taken to the web page or site associated with that image.

TIP

You can edit an image hyperlink after you have created it by selecting the image, clicking the Create Or Edit Hyperlink toolbar button, and then using the Edit Hyperlink dialog box to specify a new location.

TIP

To make a hyperlink to a file on your computer, click the File button and use the Select File dialog box to locate the file.

Create a Hyperlink to a Page in the Current Web

1. Select the image by clicking it.

2. Click the Create Or Edit Hyperlink toolbar button.

3. Use the list box to locate the web page.

4. Click OK.

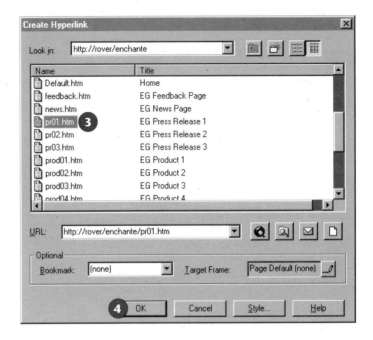

Create a Link to an Internet Resource

1 Select the image by clicking it.

2 Click the Create Or Edit Hyperlink toolbar button.

3 Type the URL of the Internet source in the URL box, or click the World Wide Web button to use your browser to locate the Internet source.

4 Click OK.

Test the Link to an Image

1 Click the Preview tab in FrontPage Editor.

2 Click the image with the hyperlink. FrontPage should display the page to which you linked the image.

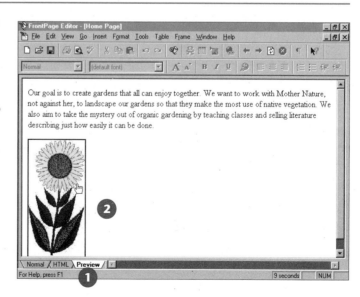

Working with Image Hotspots

Although most image hyperlinks point to a single URL address, it's possible to use an image to point to multiple URL addresses by creating hotspots. You might, for example, have an image showing a map of a state and use each region or county as a hotspot. By clicking within a particular county's borders, for instance, you could display a web page about that county.

TRY THIS

A hotspot prerequisite. *If your Internet service provider does not have FrontPage Server Extensions installed on his or her server, your image map hotspots will not work properly. To work around this problem, choose the Tools menu's Web Settings command in FrontPage Explorer. Click the Advanced tab, and select a different image map style for the image maps from the drop-down list box.*

Create a Hotspot Hyperlink

1. Select the image by clicking it.

2. Click the Rectangle, Circle, or Polygon button on the Image toolbar.

3. Click and drag within the image to create a hotspot. FrontPage Editor displays the Create Hyperlink dialog box.

4. Use the list box to locate the page to which you want the hotspot to link, or use the URL box and the buttons beside the box to create a link to a new page or a page outside the current web site.

5. Click OK.

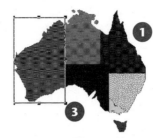

Move a Hotspot

1. Select the image by clicking it.

2. Select the hotspot by clicking the outline.

3. Drag the hotspot to the new location.

Select a Hotspot

1 Select the image by clicking it.

2 Click the Highlight Hotspots toolbar button. The image will turn white, and the hotspots will be outlined in gray.

3 Select the hotspot by clicking it.

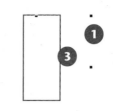

Resize a Hotspot

1 Select the image by clicking it.

2 Select the hotspot by clicking the outline.

3 Drag a selection handle to enlarge or shrink the hotspot.

Delete a Hotspot

1 Select the image by clicking it.

2 Select the hotspot by clicking the outline.

3 Press the Delete key.

Editing Hotspot Hyperlinks

It is important to periodically check all the links you add to your web pages for the obvious reason that you don't want to mislead your web visitors. If you find that a hotspot hyperlink points to the wrong page, you can edit the hyperlink so that it leads to the correct location. Then once you have made your changes, you can test the new hyperlink before publishing the web site.

SEE ALSO

For more information on URLs, see pages 90–91.

Edit a Hotspot's Link

1. Right-click the hotspot you want to relink.

2. Choose the shortcut menu's Image Hotspot Properties command.

3. Use the list box to select a different page to which you want the hotspot to link, or use the URL box and the buttons beside the box to create a link to a new page or a page outside the current web site.

4. Click OK.

TIP

If your hyperlink description isn't complete, FrontPage Editor tells you that your URL address is bad.

TIP

You can see the embedded hyperlink in the status bar. Move your pointer over the image and look at the lower left corner of your screen. The hyperlink will display.

Test the Link to a Hotspot

1 Click the Preview tab in FrontPage Editor.

2 Click the hotspot. FrontPage should display the page to which the hotspot points.

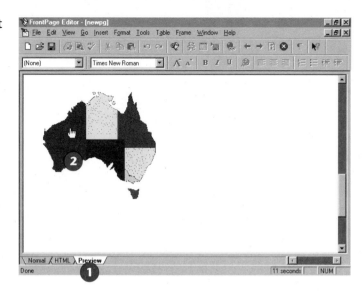

Managing Web Pages

Earlier in Section 3, "Working with Web Page Text," and Section 4, "Working with Web Page Images," this book described how you create textual and graphic content to fill your web pages with information. This section takes a slightly different tack. It describes how you use Microsoft FrontPage Editor to work with the web pages themselves: how to save web pages and later open them, how to format web pages (rather than the information on the pages), how to print web pages, and how to create links between pages.

Opening Web Pages

To work with an individual web page, you first need to open the web page. The Microsoft FrontPage applications provide a variety of ways to do this. Which method you choose depends on what you're already doing and what you want to do next.

SEE ALSO

For more information about starting FrontPage Explorer and using it to open web sites, refer to pages 6 and 10.

Open a Web Page Using Microsoft FrontPage Explorer

1 Start FrontPage, and open the web site. This starts FrontPage Explorer.

2 Double-click the web page you want to open. This starts FrontPage Editor and opens the selected web page.

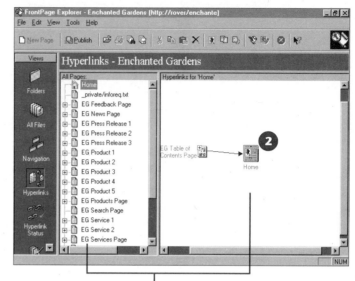

Double-click a page in either view to open the page

Open a Web Page from the Current Web Site Using FrontPage Editor

1 If FrontPage Editor is already running, click the Open toolbar button.

2 Double-click the web page you want to open.

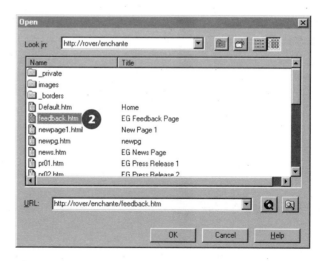

Open a Web Page from Another Location or Web Site Using FrontPage Editor

1 If FrontPage Editor is already running, click the Open toolbar button.

2 Enter the web page's location on your computer or on the World Wide Web in the URL text box. Or click the File button to browse your computer for the page, or click the World Wide Web button to browse the web for the page.

3 Click OK.

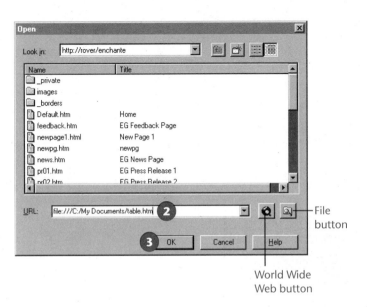

File button

World Wide Web button

5

Opening the HTML Documents Associated with Web Pages

If you know hypertext markup language (HTML), you can edit the HTML code that FrontPage creates for your web pages.

TIP

About HTML. *Web pages are stored as HTML documents. On personal computers running Microsoft Windows, HTML files use the HTM file extension. On other computers, HTML documents may use HTML as the file extension. FrontPage Editor creates the HTML instructions for your web documents automatically, so you don't have to edit them unless you want to.*

TIP

The color coding allows you to easily identify and differentiate between HTML tags, names, values, and content.

Edit a Web Page's HTML Document

1 Open the web page whose HTML code you want to edit.

2 Click the HTML tab in FrontPage Editor.

3 Edit the HTML code.

4 Click the Normal tab to continue editing the web page in FrontPage Editor, or click the Preview tab to preview your changes.

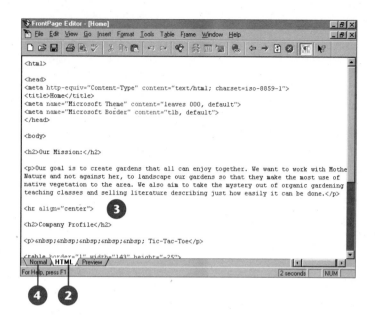

Previewing Web Pages

Before you publish a web site on the World Wide Web or even on a local network, you'll want to preview each of the web site's pages to make sure that they really will look the way you expect them to. You'll also want to preview the pages in several different browsers, because different browsers will display the same pages differently. In order to preview your web pages in different browsers, you must first obtain copies of these browsers and then install them on your computer.

TIP

If at all possible, purchase a variety of browsers, both old and new versions, from several companies. This way, you can accommodate the browsing capacities of a greater percentage of your viewers.

Preview a Web Page in FrontPage Editor

1 Open the web page you want to preview in FrontPage Editor.

2 Click the Preview tab.

3 Click the Normal tab to edit your page.

Preview a Web Page in a Browser

1 Open the web page you want to preview in FrontPage Editor.

2 Click the Preview In Browser toolbar button.

5

Navigating Web Pages

You can navigate web pages from within FrontPage Editor in many of the same ways that you can by using a web browser such as Microsoft Internet Explorer. You can move to a previously viewed web page. You can stop loading a particular web page you've requested from the web server. And you can retrieve an updated copy of a web page from the web server.

TIP

More about web page navigation. *The Refresh and Stop buttons that FrontPage Editor provides work the same way as the Refresh and Stop buttons that your web browser provides. When you refresh a web page, for example, you retrieve a new copy of the web page from the web site. When you stop loading a web page, you tell FrontPage Editor to stop loading the requested web page and to instead continue displaying the current web page.*

Move to a Previously Viewed Web Page

1. Click the Back button to move backward to the web page you just viewed.

2. Click the Forward button to move forward to the web page you were viewing before you clicked the Back button.

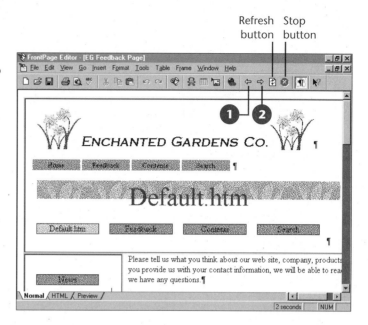

Refresh button   Stop button

Using Bookmarks

Bookmarks make it easy to move around within a particular web page or to more precisely control where visitors land when they move to the page. Bookmarks, then, work as navigation tools you use within a web page—just as hyperlinks work as navigation tools you use between web pages.

Create a Bookmark

1. Open the web page in which you want to place the bookmark.
2. Click to place the insertion point where you want to place the bookmark.
3. Choose the Edit menu's Bookmark command.
4. Type a name for the bookmark in the Bookmark Name text box.
5. Click OK.

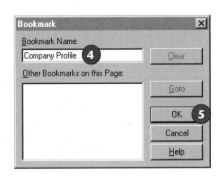

Move to a Bookmark

1. Open the web page with the bookmark.
2. Choose the Edit menu's Bookmark command.
3. Select the bookmark from the Other Bookmarks On This Page list box.
4. Click the Goto button.

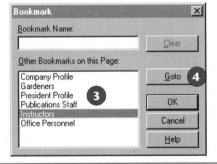

Remove an Existing Bookmark

1. Open the web page with the bookmark.
2. Choose the Edit menu's Bookmark command.
3. Double-click the bookmark in the Other Bookmarks On This Page list box.
4. Click the Clear button.

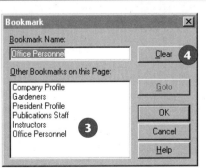

5

Linking Web Pages in the Current Web Site

Apart from playing an essential role in helping people navigate through the vastness of cyberspace, hyperlinks also have an important function on a smaller level: to link the pages within a web site. Generous use of hyperlinks between pages in a web site makes moving between the pages less of a maze to visitors, which in turn makes visitors more inclined to visit your web site again.

SEE ALSO

For more information on what frames are and how you use them, see Section 7, "Using Frames."

TIP

To edit an existing hyperlink, right-click the hyperlink and choose the shortcut menu's Hyperlink Properties command.

Create a Hyperlink to a Web Page in the Current Web Site

1 Open the web page in which you want to place the hyperlink.

2 Select the text or image that you want to turn into a clickable hyperlink.

3 Click the Create Or Edit Hyperlink toolbar button.

4 Select the web page you want visitors to move to from the list box.

5 Optionally, select a bookmark from the Bookmark drop-down list box.

6 Optionally, enter a frame in the Target Frame text box.

7 Click OK.

Linking Web Pages to Internet Locations

Imagine for a moment what the World Wide Web would be like without hyperlinks connecting web sites together. Each time you wanted to browse a different site, you would have to know the site's URL before you could get there. Hyperlinks play a key role in the World Wide Web for a good reason: they allow visitors to move freely throughout the web. A web site without hyperlinks to other sites is like a dead end, and visitors are unlikely to seek it out as they stroll through the web.

TIP

To create a hyperlink to a file on your computer, either type the prefix file:/// and the file's complete pathname in the URL text box or click the File button to browse your computer for the file.

Create a Hyperlink to an Internet Resource

1 Open the web page in which you want to place the hyperlink.

2 Select the text or image that you want to turn into a clickable hyperlink.

3 Click the Create Or Edit Hyperlink toolbar button.

4 Type the hyperlink's URL in the URL text box, or click the Use Your Web Browser To Select A Page button to locate the page.

5 Optionally, enter a frame in the Target Frame text box.

6 Click OK.

To create a hyperlink that sends e-mail, click the E-mail button and enter the e-mail address in the dialog box FrontPage provides.

To link text or an image to a new page that you want to create, click the New Page button and then use the New dialog box to describe the new page.

5

Internet Protocols and URLs

When you create hyperlinks, FrontPage asks you questions about Internet resource protocols and uniform resource locators (URLs). These questions aren't difficult to answer once you've worked a bit with the Internet; however, it's helpful for new users to get a quick overview of exactly what these things are and how they're used.

What Are Internet Protocols?

The word *protocol* is used in a variety of ways when talking about computers and the Internet. It's important for you, as a web publisher, to think about the word as a way to refer to specific sets of rules for moving information between computers. For example, the World Wide Web uses one set of rules—called the hypertext transfer protocol, or http://—for moving information from computer to computer, but the Internet actually uses several other popular protocols for moving information as well, as described in the table shown here.

Because the Internet uses or supports the use of different protocols, FrontPage Editor lets you create hyperlinks that use protocols in addition to http://. To create a hyperlink based on a different protocol, all you do is type the protocol in the URL box. The following table lists examples of protocols you might enter.

INTERNET PROTOCOLS	
Protocol	**What it does**
ftp://	Moves files between computers
gopher://	Organizes information (in the form of programs and documents) into a huge set of cascading menus
https://	Securely moves web pages between computers so that the information can't be viewed or read by other computers during transmission.
news:	Connects your web browser to a news, or newsgroup, server
telnet://	Turns your computer into a dumb computer terminal and then connects this dumb terminal to another computer—typically a large mainframe computer

How URLs Work

Uniform resource locators, or URLs, describe the precise location of an Internet or intranet resource—usually a document or program that you want to use, read, or retrieve. For example, the following is the URL for a page at the Microsoft Corporation web site:

http://www.microsoft.com/kb/deskapps/excel/q150990.htm.

In general, when you create a hyperlink—especially those that describe Internet resources rather than intranet resources—you supply three pieces of information:

◆ protocol

◆ server name

◆ file pathname

The first part of a URL describes the protocol. For example, any World Web Wide URL can and usually should include the http:// or the https:// protocol prefix. However, as discussed earlier in this sidebar, you can also create URLs that point to Internet and intranet resources in addition to web sites and web pages. (See the table on page 90 for a partial list of these other resources.)

The second part of a URL names the server where a particular resource resides. This may seem unnecessarily complicated if you're used to working in a personal computer environment, but, in general, remember that sharing information across the Internet or even a small intranet requires two computers or computer networks: a client computer or network (probably your desktop computer) and a server computer or network (the computer or network supplying the resource you want). When you want to get information from the Internet or an intranet, therefore, you need to give the client computer the name of the server computer from which it's supposed to request the information. If you wanted to grab information from the Microsoft Corporation web site, for example, you would need to supply the web server's name: www.microsoft.com

The third and final part of a URL is the file pathname. This last bit of information specifies both the document or program filename and its location on the server. In the case of the http://www.microsoft.com/ kb/deskapps/excel/q150990.htm URL, for example, kb/deskapps/excel/q150990.htm is the file pathname because the HTML document, q150990.htm, resides in the server's kb/deskapps/excel/ directory.

5

Preparing to Print Web Pages

Unlike word processing documents, which are by definition well-suited for printing on paper, the web pages you create in FrontPage are primarily designed for posting on a web. Nonetheless, you may want to have printed copies of your web pages. Luckily, FrontPage makes it easy to print your web pages. Before you click the Print button, however, you need to specify how you want your web pages to fit on paper (which doesn't have the same dimensions as your computer screen). You might also want to preview your web pages as a last step before printing them to make sure they will print exactly the way you expect them to.

HP LaserJet
4V/4MV
PostScript

Specify How the Pages of a Web Page Document Should Print

1 Open the web page you want to print.

2 Choose the File menu's Page Setup command.

3 Type the information you want to print at the top of each page in the Header box.

4 Type the information you want to print at the bottom of each page in the Footer box.

5 Specify what size margin FrontPage Editor should use for the printed pages in the Margin boxes: Left, Right, Top, and Bottom.

6 Click OK.

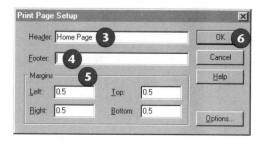

To change the paper size, print orientation, or resolution, choose the File menu's Page Setup command. Then click the Options button to access your printer's advanced settings and specify how you want your pages to print.

More about print preview. *FrontPage Editor only enables Print Preview command buttons when they make sense. For example, if there is no previous page, the Prev Page button isn't available. If there are no more pages, the Next Page button isn't available. And the Zoom Out button isn't available until you click the Zoom In button.*

Preview a Printed Web Page Document

1 Open the web page you want to print.

2 Choose the File menu's Print Preview command.

3 Click the Next Page and Prev Page buttons to move through the document you want to print.

4 Click the Two Page button to see two pages side by side in the Print Preview window. Click the One Page button—which replaces the Two Page button after you've clicked it—to display one page in the Print Preview window.

5 Click the Zoom In and Zoom Out buttons to magnify or reduce the display size of the page you want to print.

6 Click the Close button if you decide not to print the document.

7 Click the Print button if you decide to print the document.

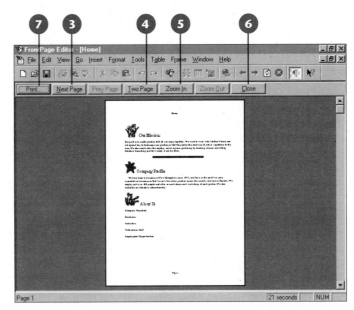

5

Printing Web Pages

You can print web pages from FrontPage Editor, and you'll probably want to do so. It's often easier to read, review, and edit web pages using printed hard-copy versions of the documents than it is to read, review, and edit pages on-screen. Any images you've placed in a web page will print as well. However, if you print a colorful web page using a one-color printer, FrontPage Editor converts colors to shades of gray.

TIP

A web page isn't equal to a single page of paper. A single web page may actually print on several pieces of paper.

Print a Web Page Document

1 Open the web page document window.

2 Choose the File menu's Print command.

3 Select the printer you want to use from the Name drop-down list box.

4 Indicate how many pages of the web page document you want to print using the Print Range buttons and boxes.

5 Specify how many copies of the web page document you want to print in the Copies box.

6 Click OK to begin printing.

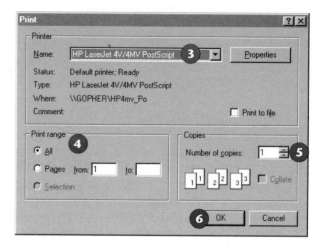

Saving Web Pages as Templates

If you create a web page design that you really like, you can save the page as a template and then use the template as a base for other pages you create.

 Enchanted Gardens Quiz

TIP

To use the web page as a replacement for an existing template, click the Browse button. Then when FrontPage Editor displays a list of the existing templates, double-click the one you want to replace with the new web page template you created.

TIP

After you save a web page as a template, the template appears in the New dialog box with the list of other web page templates and wizards.

Save a Web Page as a Template

1 Open the web page you want to save.

2 Choose the File menu's Save As command.

3 Type the filename you want to use for the web page document in the URL text box. This is the actual filename of the HTML document.

4 Type a name for the web page document in the Title text box.

5 Click the As Template button.

6 Describe the template in greater detail in the Description box—perhaps why you've created the template or for what purposes the template can be used.

7 Click OK.

8 If you don't want to save some of the images on the page along with the HTML document, select the images you don't want to save and click the Set Action button. Then click the Don't Save option button.

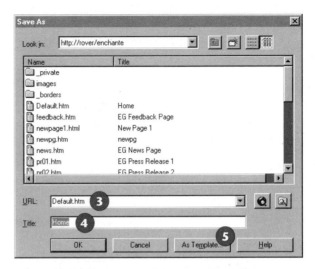

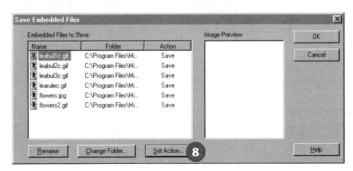

Saving Web Pages as Files

You can control when pages are saved and where they are saved by using the File menu's Save commands. If you choose the File menu's Save or Save All commands and you haven't previously saved a web page, FrontPage Editor walks you through the steps for saving a web page for the first time. As part of the process of saving a web page for the first time, you need to name the web page document, give it a filename, and indicate whether you want any of the images displayed on the web page to be saved with the HTML document.

TIP

You don't need to include the HTM file extension when you name the file. FrontPage Editor adds it for you.

Save a Web Page

1 Open the web page document window.

2 Choose the File menu's Save As command.

3 Specify where you want FrontPage Editor to save the file using the list box of folders.

4 Type the filename you want to use for the web page document in the URL text box. This is the actual filename of the HTML document.

5 Type a name for the web page document in the Title text box.

6 Click OK.

7 When FrontPage Editor asks, specify any images that you don't want saved in the HTML document by selecting the image and clicking the Set Action button. Then click the Don't Save option button.

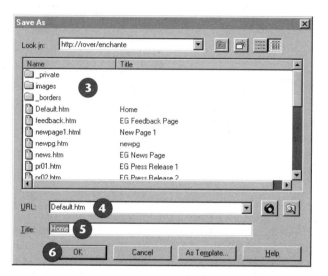

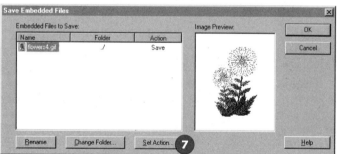

Saving images. *When FrontPage Editor asks if you want to save the images associated with the HTML document, it assumes you want the images saved in the same location as the HTML document. If you want to save the images in some other location, click the Change Folder button in the Save Embedded Files dialog box. Then use the next dialog box that FrontPage Editor displays to specify where the images should be saved.*

To save a web page a second or subsequent time, click the Save toolbar button.

Save All the Web Pages in a Web Site

1 Open the web page document window.

2 Choose the File menu's Save All command.

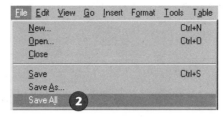

5

Tables

Some of the information you may want to include on your web pages might not fit neatly into paragraphs of text or simple lists. In these situations, you'll need to reorganize your information so that it does fit concisely and legibly on a page. One of the most practical tools available to you is a table, which presents information using a grid of columns and rows. Microsoft FrontPage Editor lets you create tables for your web pages with ease and speed.

A Few Words on Table Basics

Tables aren't difficult to use or understand. In fact, if you're a regular user of Microsoft Word or Microsoft Excel, you already know most of what you need to know. But let's quickly cover the basics.

Tables arrange information into columns and rows of data. Each column-row intersection is called a cell. You use cells to hold the table data. Table cells can hold a variety of data: text, numeric values, images, and even other tables.

The Parts of a Table

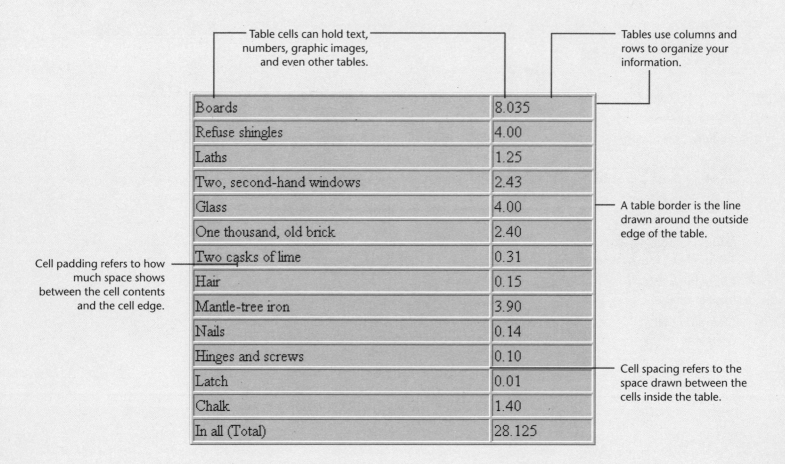

Table cells can hold text, numbers, graphic images, and even other tables.

Tables use columns and rows to organize your information.

Boards	8.035
Refuse shingles	4.00
Laths	1.25
Two, second-hand windows	2.43
Glass	4.00
One thousand, old brick	2.40
Two casks of lime	0.31
Hair	0.15
Mantle-tree iron	3.90
Nails	0.14
Hinges and screws	0.10
Latch	0.01
Chalk	1.40
In all (Total)	28.125

A table border is the line drawn around the outside edge of the table.

Cell padding refers to how much space shows between the cell contents and the cell edge.

Cell spacing refers to the space drawn between the cells inside the table.

Creating Tables

To create a table, you first need to open the web page in which you want to place the table. Once you've done this, you're ready to use the Table menu's commands and a variety of other techniques to create the table and then fill it with data.

TIP

Microsoft FrontPage 98 has a Table toolbar that often comes in handy when working with tables. To view the Table toolbar, choose the View menu's Table Toolbar command.

Insert a Table

1 Choose the Table menu's Insert Table command.

2 Describe the table.

◆ Specify the number of rows.

◆ Specify the number of columns.

3 Click OK.

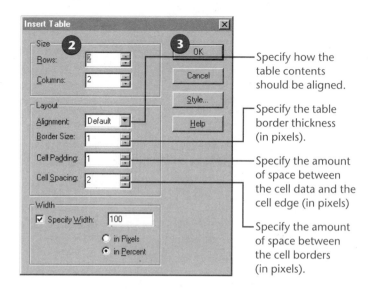

Specify how the table contents should be aligned.

Specify the table border thickness (in pixels).

Specify the amount of space between the cell data and the cell edge (in pixels)

Specify the amount of space between the cell borders (in pixels).

Draw a Table

1 Choose the Table menu's Draw Table command.

2 Drag the mouse from the point where you want the top left corner of the table to the point where you want the bottom right corner of the table.

3 Drag the mouse from one side of the table to the other to create rows or from top to bottom to create columns.

4 Click the Draw Table button on the Table toolbar when you're finished drawing the table.

Adding Cells to Tables

After you've created a table, you need to add another cell or two or even entire rows or columns of cells to accommodate more information. You can quickly accomplish all three of these tasks using the Table menu's insertion commands.

TIP

When FrontPage Editor inserts a new cell in a table, it moves the other cells in the row to the right.

TIP

If you want to insert a row above the selected row, click the Above Selection option button.

Insert a New Cell in a Table

1 Click a cell in the row and column where you want to insert the new cell.

2 Place the insertion point where you want the new cell to be inserted.

3 Choose the Table menu's Insert Cell command.

Insert a New Row in a Table

1 Click a cell in the row above where you want to insert the new row.

2 Choose the Table menu's Insert Rows Or Columns command.

3 Select the Rows option, if necessary.

4 Type the number of rows you want to insert in the Number Of Rows box.

5 Select the Below Selection option, if necessary.

6 Click OK.

January	February	April
May	June	July
August	September	October

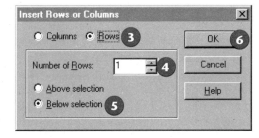

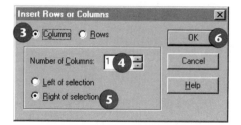

TIP

If you want to insert a column to the left of the selected column, click the Left Of Selection option button.

Insert a New Column in a Table

1 Click a cell in the column to the left of where you want to insert the new column.

2 Choose the Table menu's Insert Rows Or Columns command.

3 Select the Columns option, if necessary.

4 Type the number of columns you want to insert in the Number Of Columns box.

5 Select the Right Of Selection option, if necessary.

6 Click OK.

TIP

Just as when you inserted your first table, you can specify how cell contents should be aligned in the table-within-a-table, what size border you want around the table, what cell padding and spacing you want, and whether the table has a minimum width.

Insert a Table in a Table

1 Click the cell where you want to insert the table-within-a-table.

2 Choose the Table menu's Insert Table command.

3 Type the number of rows you want in the Rows box.

4 Type the number of columns you want in the Columns box.

5 Click OK.

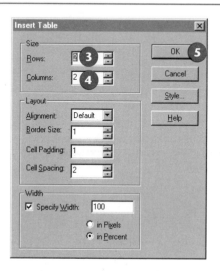

6

Combining and Splitting Cells

Sometimes you might want the contents of a single cell to span across two or more cells. Or you might want to divide a single cell into two or more cells to better fit the data you're showing in a table. To combine and split cells in situations like these, you use the Table menu's Merge Cells and Split Cells commands.

TIP

When you combine table cells, FrontPage Editor places the contents of each of the original cells onto a separate line of the new cell.

TRY THIS

You can also select a range of cells by clicking on one corner of the range and dragging the mouse to the opposite corner.

Combine Two or More Cells

1 Click the first cell you want to combine with another cell (or cells).

2 Choose the Table menu's Select Cell command.

3 While holding down the Ctrl key, click the cell (or cells) you want to combine with the cell selected in step 1.

4 Choose the Table menu's Merge Cells command.

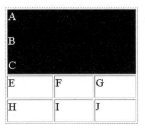

Split a Cell into Two or More Cells

1 Click the first cell you want to split into two or more cells.

2 Choose the Table menu's Split Cells command.

3 Click the Split Into Columns or Split Into Rows option button to indicate how you want to split the cell.

4 Specify how many columns or rows the selected cell should be split into in the Number Of Columns box.

5 Click OK.

Creating Table Captions

A table caption tells the viewer exactly what you're trying to represent in the table. Table captions also provide a name to use when referencing the table

TRY THIS

To move a caption to the bottom of the table, right-click the caption and then choose the shortcut menu's Caption Properties command. When FrontPage Editor displays the Caption Properties dialog box, click the Bottom Of Table option button.

Insert a Caption

1. Click the table you want to label with a caption.

2. Choose the Table menu's Insert Caption command.

3. Type the caption you want to use to label the table.

Delete a Caption

1. Click to the left of the caption text.

2. Press the Delete key.

3. Select the (now empty) line by clicking to the left of the line.

4. Press the Delete key.

Deleting Cells from Tables

After you've filled in your table, you might find that you created it with one or two columns or rows too many. This is easy to fix, however, by deleting the row, column, or individual cell from the table. If you are unsatisfied with your table altogether, you can delete the entire table. Likewise, you can delete an entire table from within a table.

> **TIP**
>
> *You can also choose the Table menu's Delete Cells command to delete the selected cell.*

> **TIP**
>
> *You can also use the Delete Cells button on the Table toolbar to delete the selected cells.*

Delete a Cell

1 Click the cell you want to delete.

2 Choose the Table menu's Select Cell command.

3 Press the Delete key.

Monday	Tuesday	Wednesday
Thursday	Friday	**Purple** ❶

This is how the table looks before the cell deletion.

Monday	Tuesday	Wednesday
Thursday	Friday	

This is how the table looks after the cell deletion.

Selecting rows and columns with a mouse. *You can also select table rows and columns using the mouse. To select a row with the mouse, point to the row's left border and then click the border when you see the pointer turn into a black arrow. To select a column with the mouse, point to the column's top border and then click the border when you see the pointer turn into a black arrow.*

Delete a Row, Column, or Table

1. Click a cell in the row or column you want to delete. Or just click any cell if you want to delete the table.

2. Choose the appropriate selection command from the Table menu:

   ◆ Choose Select Row to select a row for deletion

   ◆ Choose Select Column to select a column for deletion

   ◆ Choose Select Table to select the entire table for deletion.

3. Press the Delete key.

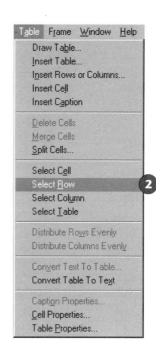

Filling a Table with Information

Once you've created a table to hold your information, you're ready to begin filling the individual table cells with text, numbers, and even images. This process works very much like you might expect. You click the cell in which you want to place information. Then you enter that information.

Enter Text or a Number in a Table Cell

1 Click the table cell.

2 Type the text or number you want in the cell.

Boards	8.035
Refuse shingles	4.00
Laths	1.25
Two, second-hand windows	2.43
Glass	4.00
One thousand, old brick	2.40
Two casks of lime	0.31
Hair	0.15
Mantle-tree iron	3.90
Nails	0.14
Hinges and screws	0.10
Latch	0.01
Chalk	1.40
In all (Total)	28.125

Copy and Move Data Between Table Cells

1 Click the cell with the text or number you want to copy.

2 Select the cell's contents by dragging the mouse from the first character to the last character.

3 Click the Copy toolbar button to copy text. Or click the Cut toolbar button to move text.

4 Click the cell in which you want to paste the text or number.

5 Click the Paste toolbar button.

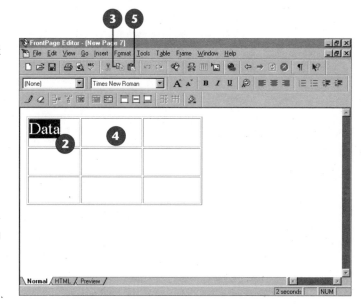

Adding Images to Tables

Tables traditionally hold textual and numerical data, but you can also include images in your tables to spruce them up a bit. You add images to table cells in the same way that you add images to any other location on a web page.

TRY THIS

To resize an image, click the image to select it. Then drag the selection handles.

Insert an Image in a Table Cell

1 Click the table cell.

2 Click the Insert Image toolbar button.

3 Double-click the Images folder to display a list of the images you've already placed (or that FrontPage has already placed) in the web site's pages.

4 Double-click the image you want to insert.

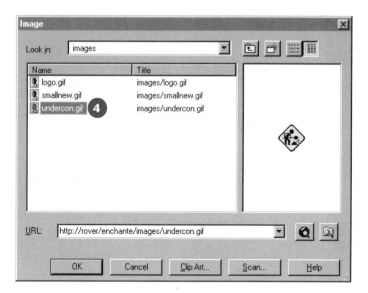

Insert a Clip Art Image in a Table Cell

1 Click the table cell.

2 Click the Insert Image toolbar button.

3 Click the Clip Art button.

4 Select a clip art category from the Category list box.

5 Double-click the clip art image you want to insert.

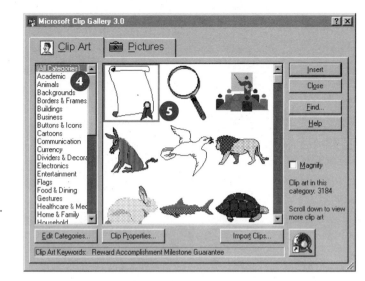

Copying and Moving Images in Tables

Just as you can copy and move textual and numerical information between cells in tables, you can also move images between table cells.

Copy or Move an Image Between Table Cells

1 Click the cell with the image you want to copy or move.

2 Select the image by clicking it.

3 Click the Copy toolbar button to copy the image. Or click the Cut toolbar button to move the image.

4 Click the cell in which you want to paste the image.

5 Click the Paste toolbar button.

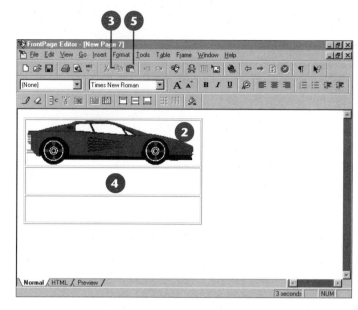

Deleting Cell Contents

If you erroneously enter contents in a cell, you can easily edit the contents or delete them completely.

Delete Text or Numbers in a Table Cell

1. Click the cell with the text or number you want to remove.

2. Select the cell's contents by dragging the mouse from the first character to the last character.

3. Press the Delete key.

Delete an Image in a Table Cell

1. Click the cell with the image you want to remove.

2. Select the image by clicking it.

3. Press the Delete key.

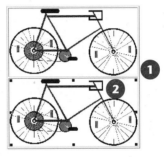

6

Changing a Table's Layout

After you've created a table and filled it with information, you'll probably want to make changes to the table's appearance. Fortunately, this isn't difficult to do because FrontPage Editor gives you control over the appearance of your tables. For instance, if your table lists numerical data, you might want to right-align the cell contents so that the digits line up. You can also change a table's border size or the spacing between the cells to make the table stand out and to make it easier to read.

TIP

You can also adjust the table border thickness by clicking the arrows in the Border Size box.

Change the Alignment of Table Cell Contents

1 Right-click the table.

2 Choose the shortcut menu's Table Properties command.

3 Activate the Alignment drop-down list box, and select the alignment you want to use: Left, Right, or Center.

4 Click OK.

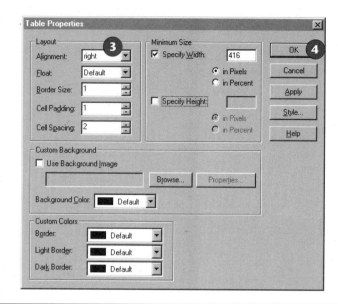

Change the Border Thickness of the Table

1 Right-click the table.

2 Choose the shortcut menu's Table Properties command.

3 Specify the table border thickness (in pixels) in the Border Size box.

4 Click OK.

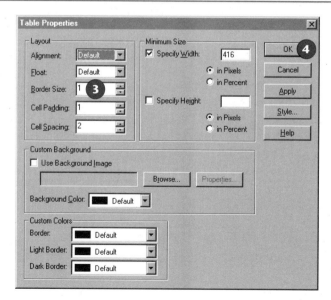

SEE ALSO

For more information about what cell spacing and cell padding are, refer to pages 100–101.

Change the Cell Size in the Table

1 Right-click the table.

2 Choose the shortcut menu's Table Properties command.

3 Specify the space inside the cells (in pixels) in the Cell Padding box.

4 Click OK.

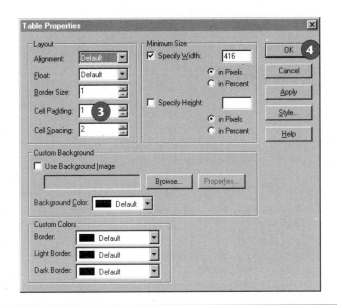

Change the Cell Spacing in the Table

1 Right-click the table.

2 Choose the shortcut menu's Table Properties command.

3 Specify the amount of space between the cell borders (in pixels) in the Cell Spacing box.

4 Click OK.

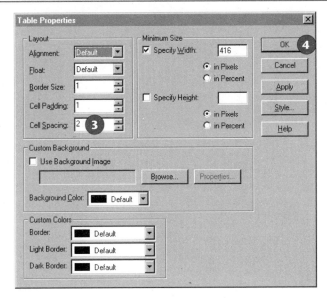

6

Changing a Table's Background

By adding color and graphic content to your tables, you can capture your visitors' attention and make your tables more exciting to look at.

Color the Table Background

1. Right-click the table.

2. Choose the shortcut menu's Table Properties command.

3. Activate the Background Color drop-down list box; then select a color.

4. Click OK.

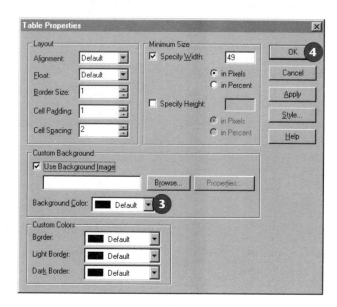

Use an Image for the Table Background

1 Right-click the table.

2 Choose the shortcut menu's Table Properties command.

3 Check the Use Background Image box.

4 Click the Browse button.

5 Select the image you want to use by double-clicking the Select Background Image dialog box.

6 Click OK.

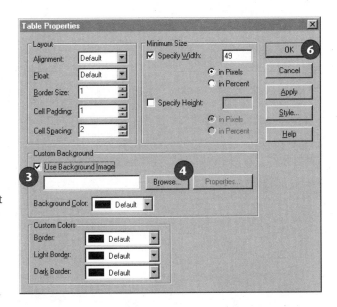

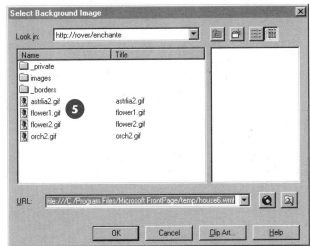

Changing a Table's Border Colors

There are two different ways you can color the borders of a table. You can color all the borders with the same color, or you can use two (preferably complementary) colors to give the table a drop-shadow effect.

TIP

The Border drop-down list box's setting has no effect on your table borders if you use the Dark Border and Light Border settings.

TIP

You use the colors specified by the Dark Border and Light Border drop-down list boxes to create the illusion of shading.

Color All the Table's Borders with One Color

1. Right-click the table.

2. Choose the shortcut menu's Table Properties command.

3. Activate the Border drop-down list box; then select a color for all the table's borders.

4. Click OK.

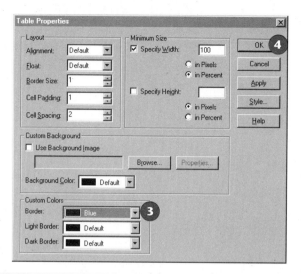

Color the Table's Borders with Different Colors

1. Right-click the table.

2. Choose the shortcut menu's Table Properties command.

3. Activate the Light Border drop-down list box; then select a color for the table's top and left exterior and bottom and right interior borders.

4. Activate the Dark Border drop-down list box; then select a color for the table's bottom and right exterior and top and left interior borders.

5. Click OK.

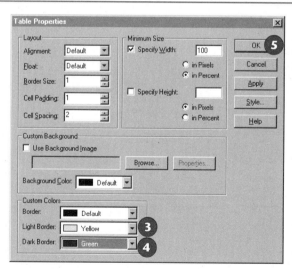

Changing a Table's Width

How well the table fits in the web page and with the rest of the page's content is yet another detail you need to consider. If possible, for example, you want to avoid making your web page visitors scroll back and forth to see the right and left sides or top and bottom of a table in your web page.

TIP

As you set your table width, keep in mind that different visitors will use different monitor sizes and desktop areas.

Change the Width of the Table

1 Right-click the table.

2 Choose the shortcut menu's Table Properties command.

3 Check the Specify Width box.

4 To specify the table width in pixels, click the In Pixels option button. Then enter a value in the text box.

5 To specify the table width as a percentage of the web page width, click the In Percent option button. Then enter a value in the text box.

6 Click OK.

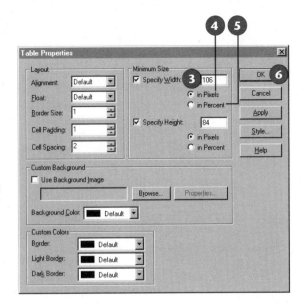

Changing Cell Width and Layout

Just as you can change the layout of an entire table, you can also change the layout of individual cells in a table. To fit a large amount of information into a single cell, for example, you can increase the width of the cell. You can right-align numbers in cells and left-align or center textual content. You can also create column and row headers to describe the labels and values included in your table.

> **TIP**
>
> *Horizontal alignment refers to how the cell contents fit between the cell's left and right edges. Vertical alignment refers to how the cell contents fit between the cell's top and bottom edges.*

> **TIP**
>
> *Consider the number of columns in your table as you set the cell width. For example, if you have two columns, you might want each column to take up half or slightly less than half of the web page's width.*

Change the Width and Alignment of a Cell

1. Right-click the cell.

2. Choose the shortcut menu's Cell Properties command.

3. Activate the Horizontal Alignment drop-down list box; then select the horizontal alignment for the cell's contents: Left, Center, or Right.

4. Activate the Vertical Alignment drop-down list box; then select the vertical alignment for the cell's contents: Top, Middle, Baseline, or Bottom.

5. Check the Specify Width box, and enter a value in the text box.

6. Click OK.

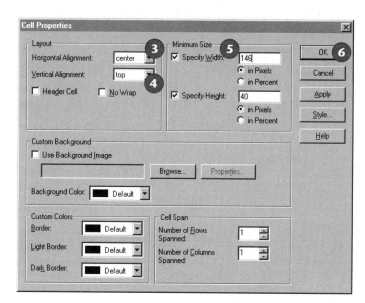

To create a row of header cells, click a cell in the row, choose the Table menu's Select Row command, and then complete the steps for Create a Header Cell. To create a column of header cells, click a cell in the column, choose the Table menu's Select Column command, and then complete the steps for Create a Header Cell.

Create a Header Cell

1 Right-click the cell.

2 Choose the shortcut menu's Cell Properties command.

3 Check the Header Cell box.

4 To specify that cell contents shouldn't wrap—or shouldn't break onto separate lines—check the No Wrap box.

5 Click OK.

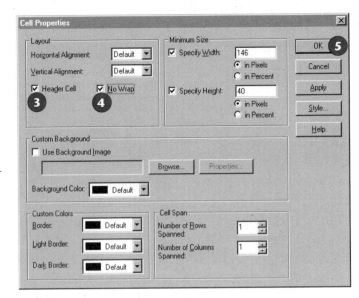

Changing a Cell's Background

Changing the background color of individual cells can be used to good effect in your tables. You could, for instance, choose a brightly colored background for a single cell to draw attention to it.

SEE ALSO

For more information about the Select Background Image dialog box, refer to page 117.

Color the Cell Background

1. Right-click the cell.

2. Choose the shortcut menu's Cell Properties command.

3. Activate the Background Color drop-down list box; then select a color.

4. Click OK.

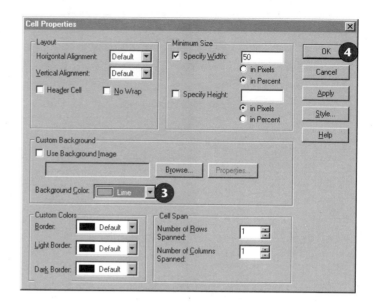

Use an Image for the Cell Background

1. Right-click the cell.

2. Choose the shortcut menu's Cell Properties command.

3. Check the Use Background Image box.

4. Click the Browse button.

5. Select the image you want to use from the Select Background Image dialog box.

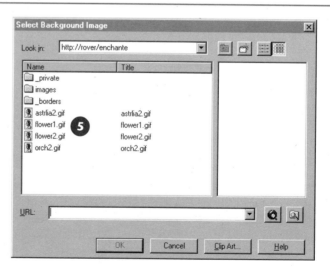

Changing Cell Border Colors

As with coloring the borders of an entire table, you have two options for recoloring the borders of a single cell. You can color all sides of the cell with the same color, or you can choose two colors to give the cell a shadow effect.

TIP

The Cell Properties dialog box's border settings override the Table Properties dialog box's border settings.

Color the Cell Border with One Color

1 Right-click the cell.

2 Choose the shortcut menu's Cell Properties command.

3 Activate the Border drop-down list box; then select a color for the cell's border.

4 Click OK.

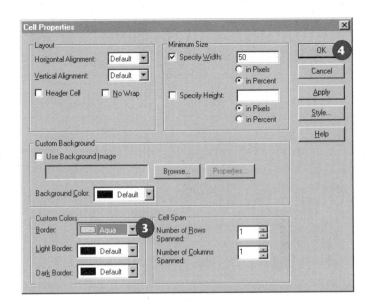

Color the Cell Border with Different Colors

1 Right-click the cell.

2 Choose the shortcut menu's Cell Properties command.

3 Activate the Light Border drop-down list box; then select a color for the cell's bottom and right borders.

4 Activate the Dark Border drop-down list box; then select a color for the cell's top and left borders.

5 Click OK.

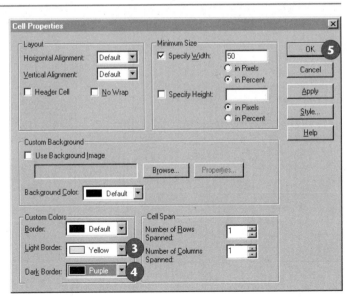

6

Changing Cell Span

If the information in one cell applies to several cells in a row or column (as is often the case with header cells), you might want to stretch the cell to span the row or column rather than retyping the same information in each cell. By doing so, you not only save yourself time but also simplify your table.

TIP

Typically, a cell spans, or occupies, a single row or single column of a table.

Stretch the Cell to Span Multiple Rows

1 Right-click the cell.

2 Choose the shortcut menu's Cell Properties command.

3 Specify how many rows and columns this cell should span in the Number Of Rows Spanned and Number Of Columns Spanned boxes.

4 Click OK.

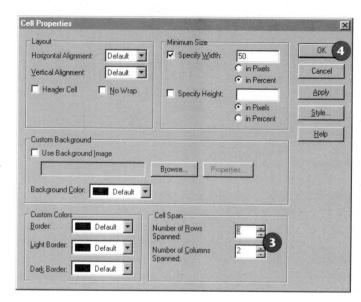

Using Frames

Frames pages let you divide a web browser window into a set of "windowpanes," or frames, and thereby give you the ability to show more than one HTML document at a time. For example, you might use one frame to show your web site's table of contents while using the other frame to show the different web pages requested by the web site visitor.

To create a frames page, you describe a grid of frames that you want a web browser to display. Then for each frame, you provide a hyperlink to the HTML document—the actual web page—which the web browser should display in that frame.

The frames page itself is just another HTML document. To display a frames page, a visitor simply clicks a hyperlink to the frames page. Or a visitor can indirectly request the frames page, such as by visiting a web site for which the frames page is the Home page. Once a visitor requests (either directly or indirectly) to load a frames page, the web server passes the frames page to the visitor's web browser and then passes the individual HTML documents—the target frames—that will fill the frames of the frames page.

Creating Frames Pages

You can create a frames page using the Frame menu's New Frames Page command. The New Frames Page command lets you choose from a rich set of templates that show how you might organize a frames page. Once you have created the frames page, you can then specify which web pages go in the frames.

Create a Frames Page

1 Start FrontPage Editor.

2 Choose the Frame menu's New Frames Page command.

3 Select a template from the list box.

4 Click OK.

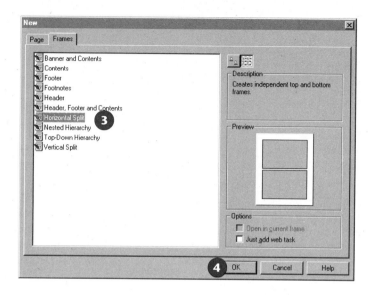

Add a New Page to a Frame

1 Open the frames page.

2 Click a frame.

3 Click the New Page button.

4 Add text, images, and hyperlinks to the new page.

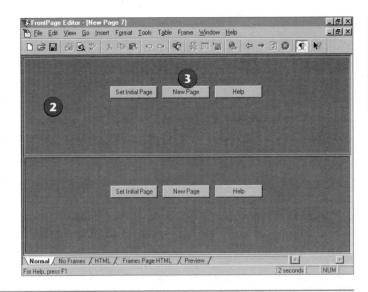

TIP

Click the File button in the Create Hyperlink dialog box to browse your computer for the initial page.

Add an Existing Page to a Frame

1 Open the frames page.

2 Click a frame.

3 Click the Set Initial Page button.

4 Select the page you want to add from the Create Hyperlink dialog box FrontPage displays.

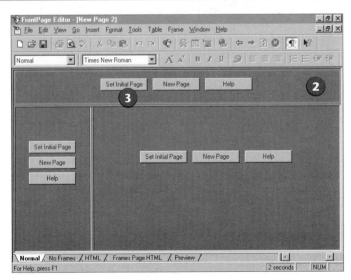

Saving Pages in a Frames Page

If you add new pages to a frames page, you can save them using the Frame menu's Save Page As command. This command works in the same basic way as the File menu's Save As command.

TIP

The name that you enter in the URL box becomes the filename of the HTML document. The title you enter in the Title box appears at the top of the web browser window when the frames page is displayed.

Save a Page

1. Choose the Frame menu's Save Page As command.

2. Type a name for the page in the URL text box.

3. Type a title for the page in the Title text box.

4. Click OK.

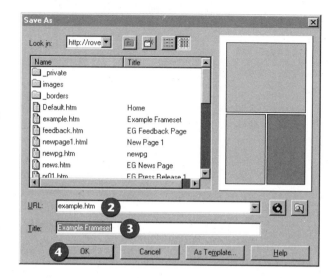

Splitting and Deleting Frames

If the frames page that you initially create doesn't work or look the way you want, you can easily split frames into still more frames. You can also delete frames.

Split a Frame

1 Click the frame to select it.

2 Choose the Frame menu's Split Frame command.

3 Use the option buttons to specify whether you want to split the selected frame horizontally or vertically.

4 Click OK.

Delete a Frame

1 Click the frame to select it.

2 Choose the Frame menu's Delete Frame command.

Editing Frames Pages

You can edit a frames page even after you create it. For example, you can adjust or resize the frames page's grid. You can rename the frames page or change its URL. And, of course, you can create and edit the individual pages that are displayed in the frames page's frames.

SEE ALSO

For more information about adding text to web pages, refer to Section 3. For more information about adding images to web pages, refer to Section 4. For more information about creating hyperlinks, refer to pages 88–89.

Edit a Page in a Frames Page

1 Open the frames page with the page you want to edit.

2 Edit the page directly in the frame, or select the page and choose the Frame's menu's Open Page In New Window command.

3 Add text, images, and hyperlinks to the page in the usual way.

Change the Frames Page Grid

1 Open the frames page you want to change.

2 Resize the dimensions of the individual frames in the grid by dragging the gridlines.

3 Split a frame by holding down the Ctrl key and then dragging the frame gridline.

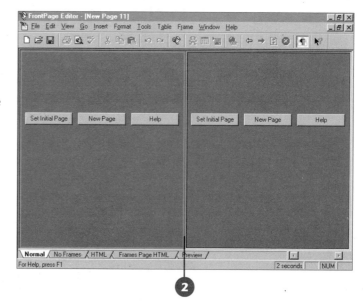

Edit the Frame Properties

1 Open the frames page with the frame you want to edit.

2 Right-click the frame, and choose the shortcut menu's Frame Properties command.

3 Type a new name or edit the existing name for the frame in the Name text box.

4 Clear the Resizable In Browser check box if you don't want web site visitors to resize the frames page's frames as they view them.

5 Use the Show Scrollbars drop-down list box to indicate whether a browser should provide scroll bars for the frame.

6 Adjust the frame margins in the Margin Width and Margin Height boxes.

7 Type a new URL or edit the existing URL for the frame in the Initial Page text box. Or click the Browse button, and then use the dialog box that FrontPage Editor displays to choose an HTML document.

8 Click OK.

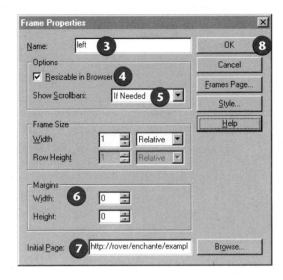

7

Specifying Target Frames

You can control what happens to a visitor's web browser window after clicking a hyperlink inside a frame. Specifically, you can control whether the new HTML document appears in the same frame, a new frame, or a new window.

TIP

If you want the target of a hyperlink to appear in the same frame as the page containing the hyperlink, click the Same Frame entry in the Common Targets list box.

TIP

You can specify a target frame for a form in the same way you specify a target frame from a page.

Specify a Target Frame for a Page

1 Choose the Frame menu's Frames Page Properties command.

2 Click the General tab.

3 Click the Default Target Frame button.

4 Select a target frame from the Common Targets list box.

5 Click OK.

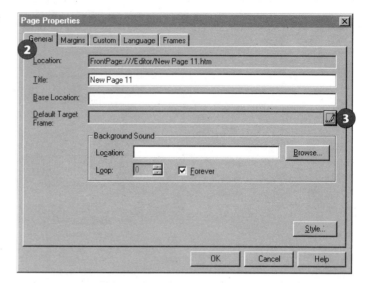

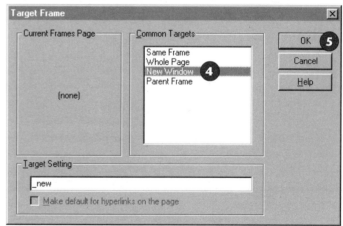

Using Special Effects

Although many web pages combine only text and images, with Microsoft FrontPage you can spice up your web pages by adding sound, background colors and images, video, and animation (in the form of movie-theater-like marquees). You need to be judicious about the manner in which you use these special effects, however, because some of them may dramatically affect the speed with which visitors access your web site. (Video clips in particular take a long time to move across networks—even local area networks.)

Nevertheless, special effects provide unique opportunities. Video clips can be a highly effective way to present different kinds of information. (A web site concentrating on early twentieth-century history might show a video clip of Winston Churchill, for example.) Sound, background colors, and background images can make your web site more dynamic or exciting. (An international travel web site might use local music to set the mood.) Marquees can help you emphasize key bits of web page information. (By using a marquee to highlight an important hyperlink, for example, you reduce the chance that visitors will miss it.) Animated buttons and advertisement banners can be used to spark the curiosity of your web site visitors. (A hover button comes alive when a visitor moves a mouse over it; banner ads spotlight new products or services.)

Using Background Colors

You'll probably want to use background colors in at least some of your web pages to make them more interesting. As you choose a background color, keep your text and link colors in mind and make sure that these colors will stand out against your background color.

TIP

If the web page uses a theme, you cannot specify a background color.

Specify a Background Color

1 Open the web page in which you want to add a background color.

2 Choose the Format menu's Background command.

3 Click the Specify Background And Colors option button.

4 Activate the Background drop-down list box; then select the background color you want to use.

5 Click OK.

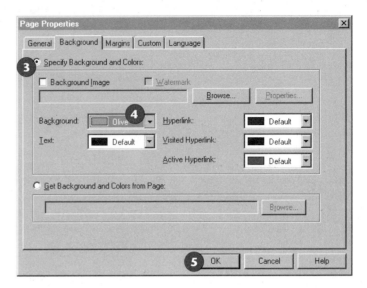

TIP

You can borrow background color only from another page in the current web site.

Borrow the Background Color from Another Page

1 Open the web page in which you want to add a background color.

2 Choose the Format menu's Background command.

3 Click the Get Background And Colors From Page option button.

4 Click the Browse button to locate the page, and then double-click the page when you find it.

5 Click OK.

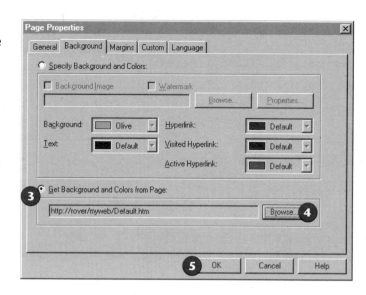

Inserting Background Images

Most of the web pages shown as examples in this book don't use background images. The reason is that in black-and-white illustrations such as those used in this book, colorful background images would produce crazy-looking, almost-impossible-to-look-at moiré patterns. On your web pages, however, you'll probably want to use background images because they can dramatically improve the visual appeal of your web site.

TIP

Check the Watermark box if you want to add a background image to the page but you don't want the image to scroll as the page scrolls.

Insert a Background Image from the Current Web

1. Open the web page in which you want to add a background image.

2. Choose the Format menu's Background command.

3. Check the Background Image box.

4. Click the Browse button.

5. Use the Select Background Image dialog box to locate the image you want to insert.

6. Click OK to insert the image.

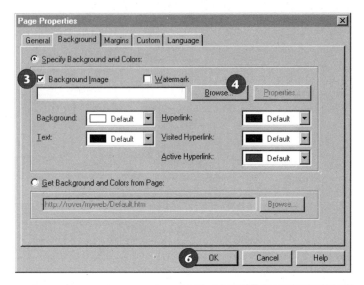

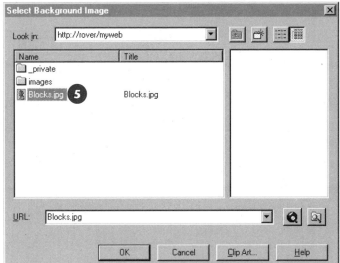

TRY THIS

Choose the Format menu's Theme command to add or change the theme of a web page. To change a web site's theme, see page 21.

Insert a Background Image from a File

1 Open the web page in which you want to add a background image.

2 Choose the Format menu's Background command.

3 Check the Background Image box.

4 Click the Browse button.

5 Click the File button.

6 Use the Select File dialog box to locate and select the image file.

7 Click Open.

8 Click OK.

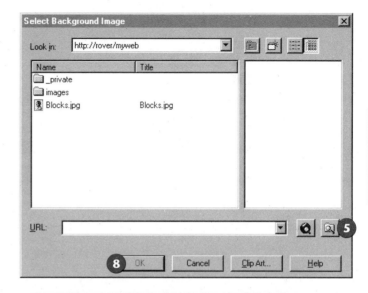

Inserting Background Images from Clip Art

In addition to creating your own background images to wallpaper your web pages, you can also choose from several existing clip art backgrounds. For the artistically not-so-inclined, these backgrounds are an easy way to add an attractive design to your web pages without overdoing the effect and making the pages a headache to read.

Use a Clip Art Background

1 Open the web page in which you want to add a background image.

2 Choose the Format menu's Background command.

3 Check the Background Image box.

4 Click the Browse button.

5 Click the Clip Art button.

6 Select a clip art category from the list box.

7 Double-click the clip art image you want to use.

8 Click OK.

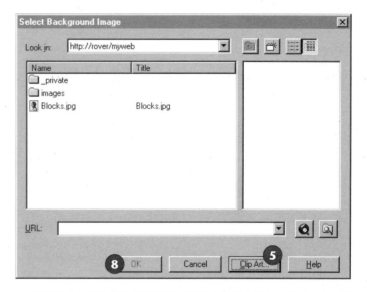

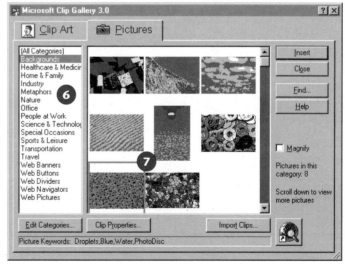

Changing Text and Link Colors

After you add a background color or image, you might need to change the text or link colors so that they can be read against the background. This is a very simple process, and the only rule of thumb to keep in mind is that the text and each of the link colors should all be unique and easily differentiated from the rest.

Change a Page's Text and Link Colors

1 Open the web page in which you want to change the text or link color.

2 Choose the Format menu's Background command.

3 Click the Specify Background And Colors option button.

4 Activate the Text, Hyperlink, Visited Hyperlink, or Active Hyperlink dropdown list boxes; then select the color you want to use for the text.

5 Click OK.

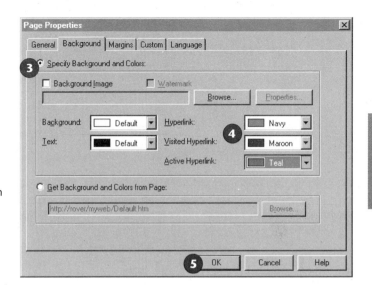

Adding Background Sound

You can add background sound to your web pages. Assuming a visitor's client computer is multimedia capable—in other words, that the visitor's desktop computer possesses a sound card and speakers—the visitor's web browser plays the background sound when the web page is loaded or refreshed.

Sounds

TIP

You need to be thoughtful about how and where you use background sound. Sound files can be very large—which means they can dramatically increase the time it takes to retrieve a page. For example, a 1-second WAV file uses about 15K of disk space and requires roughly 4 seconds of transmission time using a dial-up, 28.8-Kbps modem connection.

Insert a Background Sound

1. Open the web page in which you want to add background sound.

2. Right-click the page, and choose the shortcut menu's Page Properties command.

3. Enter the sound file's pathname in the Background Sound Location text box, or click the Browse button to locate the file.

4. To play the background sound a specified number of times when someone loads the web page, first make sure that the Forever box is not checked. If it is, remove the check. Then use the Loop box to specify how many times you want the background sound to play.

5. Click OK.

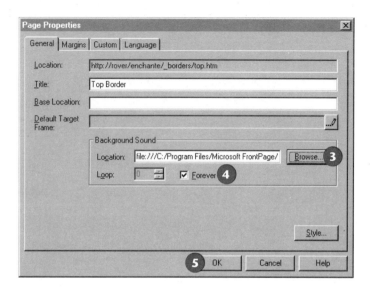

Inserting Video Clips

You can insert video clips in your web pages and control when and how a visitor sees the video clips. Note, however, that the visitor's client computer must be multimedia capable—in other words, that the visitor's desktop computer possesses a sound card and speakers—in order for the video's sound to play.

TIP

To insert a video clip from a file on your computer, click the File button and use the Select File dialog box to locate the video file.

TIP

FrontPage Editor allows you to insert video clip files that use the AVI file format.

TIP

You need to be judicious about how and where you use video clips. Video clip files can be very large—which means they can dramatically increase the time it takes to retrieve a page.

Insert a Video Clip from the Current Web

1 Open the web page in which you want to add a video clip.

2 Choose the Insert menu's Active Elements command and the Active Elements submenu's Video command.

3 Select the video clip file you want to insert.

4 Click OK.

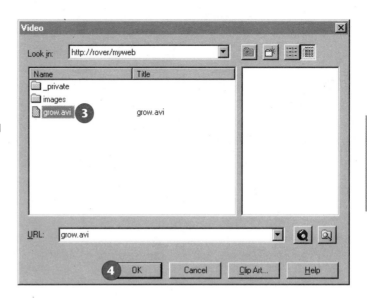

8

Changing Video Clip Properties

As with the other special effects you can add to a web page, you'll want to be judicious in your use of video clips and make sure that their inclusion in the web page doesn't defeat its purpose. Once you insert a video clip in a web page, preview the web page in a browser before publishing it. You may find that you want to change the video clip's properties to make it fit with the rest of the page.

TIP

If you want a video to play over and over, check the Forever box.

TIP

Use the General tab of the Image Properties dialog box to specify alternative representations for the video clip.

Change the Way a Video Clip Plays

1 Right-click the video clip.

2 Choose the shortcut menu's Image Properties command.

3 Click the Video tab.

4 If you want visitors who view the video clip in a browser to have clickable Play and Stop buttons, check the Show Controls In Browser box.

5 Specify the number of times you want the video to play in the Loop box.

6 If the video clip plays more than once, specify the length of time between the video clip's ending and beginning in the Loop Delay box.

7 Check a Start box to indicate when the video clip should play.

8 Click OK.

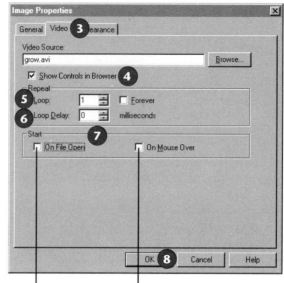

Check the On File Open box if you want the video clip to play when a visitor opens the web page.

Check the On Mouse Over box if you want the video clip to play when a visitor moves the mouse over the video clip.

Change the Layout and Appearance of a Video Clip

1. Right-click the video clip.

2. Choose the shortcut menu's Image Properties command.

3. Click the Appearance tab.

4. Specify the video clip's positioning on the web page in the Alignment drop-down list box.

5. Specify the border size around the video clip in the Border Thickness box.

6. Indicate the amount of space (in pixels) between the video clip and the web page's other content (text, images, and so forth) in the Horizontal Spacing and Vertical Spacing boxes.

7. Click OK.

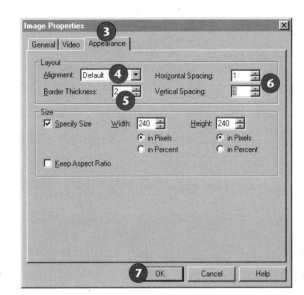

8

Resizing Video Clips

One of the most common changes made after inserting a video clip is to alter its size so that the video clip fits with the layout of the rest of the page. FrontPage Editor offers two simple ways of doing this: by using the mouse or by using commands.

Change a Video Clip's Size with the Mouse

1 Open the web page with the video clip.

2 Select the video clip.

3 Drag a corner handle to make the video clip smaller or larger.

♦ Drag a corner handle toward the center of the video clip to decrease the video's frame.

♦ Drag a corner handle away from the center of the video clip to increase the video's size.

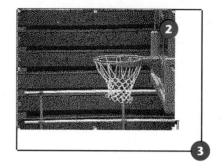

Change a Video Clip's Size with a Command

1 Right-click the video clip.

2 Choose the shortcut menu's Image Properties command.

3 Click the Appearance tab.

4 Check the Specify Size box.

5 To specify the video clip width, mark the In Pixels or In Percent option button. Then enter a value in the Width text box.

6 To specify the video clip height, select the In Pixels or the In Percent option. Then enter a value in the Height text box.

7 Click OK.

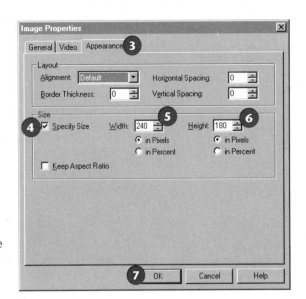

8

Creating Marquees

Another way you can add visual interest to your web pages is by creating marquees. Marquees use moving text for emphasis—the same way that some movie theaters use a marquee to tell you what movie is playing and who's starring.

TIP

Click the Style button and use the tabs in the Style dialog box to specify the marquee's font, border, and background image.

TRY THIS

To add animation effects to text, select the text and choose the Format menu's Animation command. Then choose one of the animation effects from the submenu. Animation effects can be viewed only with Microsoft Internet Explorer 4.0 or later.

Create a Marquee

1. Open the web page in which you want to add a marquee.

2. Click the line on which you want to place the marquee.

3. Choose the Insert menu's Active Elements command and the Active Elements submenu's Marquee command.

4. Type the marquee text you want to roll onto and off of the web page in the Text box.

5. Click OK.

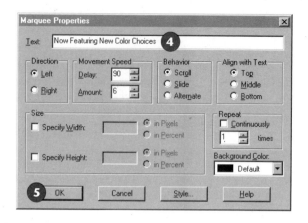

Convert an Existing Heading to a Marquee

1 Open the web page in which you want to add a marquee.

2 Select the heading you want to be a marquee.

3 Choose the Insert menu's Marquee command.

4 Click OK.

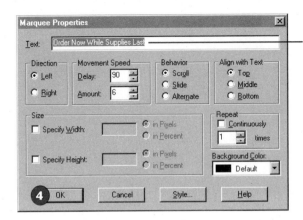

The text you selected appears here.

Customizing Marquees

After you have created a marquee, the next step is to customize the marquee to fit the page and to suit your own tastes as well. FrontPage offers several ways in which you can customize a marquee. You can change the direction and speed at which it scrolls across the screen. You can also specify the marquee's size and background color.

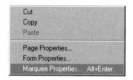

Change the Marquee's Properties

1 Right-click the marquee.

2 Choose the shortcut menu's Marquee Properties command.

3 Edit the text shown in the Text box

4 Click a Direction option button to indicate the direction in which the marquee should move: Left (to the left) or Right (to the right).

5 Specify the speed of the marquee in the Movement Speed boxes.

6 Click a Behavior option button to indicate the kind of marquee you want.

◆ Scroll lets the marquee roll onto and off of the web page.

◆ Slide lets the marquee roll onto the web page and then stop.

◆ Alternate lets the marquee roll onto and off of the web page from different directions.

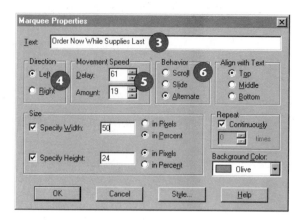

TIP

You can also change the width or height of a marquee by clicking it (to select it) and then dragging one of its selection handles.

TIP

Check the Continuously box to have a scrolling or alternating marquee run as long as the web page is being viewed. Or clear the check box, and enter the number of times you want the marquee to run in the Times box.

TIP

To delete a marquee, click it and press the Delete key.

7 Check the Specify Width box, and then set the width and specify the unit of measurement you're using.

8 Check the Specify Height box, and then set the height and specify the unit of measurement you're using.

9 Activate the Background Color drop-down list box; then select the color you want.

10 Click OK.

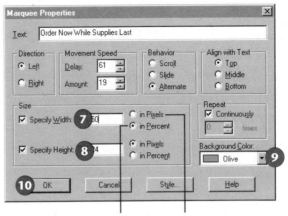

Selecting the In Percent option specifies the width or height as a percentage of the web page width or height.

Selecting the In Pixels option specifies the width or height in number of pixels

8

Inserting Animated Buttons and Advertisement Banners

FrontPage 98 allows you to easily insert two popular Java applets, hover buttons and banner ads, right from the Insert menu, so you don't have to know Java script language to use these nifty features. A hover button works in much the same way as a regular button, but it comes alive when a visitor moves the mouse over it. The banner ad manager is useful if you are creating a corporate web site including advertising. It inserts an image and then fades to another image, similar to an electronic billboard at a sports stadium.

Insert a Hover Button

1 Open the web page in which you want to insert a hover button.

2 Place the insertion point where you want to insert the button.

3 Choose the Insert menu's Active Elements command and the Active Elements submenu's Hover Button command.

4 Enter the button text.

5 Enter the page that you want displayed when a visitor clicks the Hover button, or click the Browse button to locate the page.

6 Select a button color.

7 Activate the Effect drop-down list box, and select an animation effect. Then select the color of the effect.

8 Click OK.

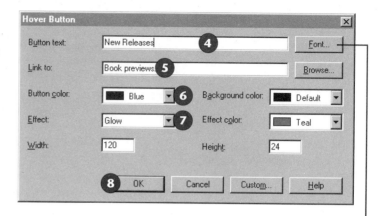

Click the Font button to specify the button text font.

Insert a Banner Ad

1. Open the web page in which you want to insert a banner ad.

2. Place the insertion point where you want to insert the banner.

3. Choose the Insert menu's Active Elements command and the Active Elements submenu's Banner Ad Manager command.

4. Specify the banner's width and height.

5. Activate the Effect drop-down list box; then select a transition effect.

6. Describe how long each advertisement should display.

7. Enter the advertising company's Home page, if appropriate.

8. Click the Add button to add images to be displayed.

9. Click OK.

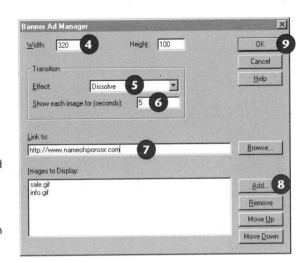

8

Inserting FrontPage Components

FrontPage Components represent a key feature of Microsoft FrontPage. People with little or no background in computer programming can use FrontPage Components to create interactive web sites and web sites that automatically update. FrontPage Components automate such tasks as displaying how many viewers have visited your web site and changing graphic images or references to HTML files on a certain date. Sophisticated FrontPage Components in form pages (described in the next section) tell the server to redisplay the information a web site visitor just entered, and simple components perform rudimentary tasks, such as inserting the designated content. Some FrontPage Components are static and wait for user input. (The Confirmation Field works this way.) Other components are dynamic and change automatically each time a visitor requests the page. (The Hit Counter works this way.)

Even if you haven't added any FrontPage Components on your own, your FrontPage web probably already includes some. If, for example, you created your web site using one of FrontPage's web wizards, FrontPage added several components for you as it created the site. You can recognize most of the FrontPage Components on your web pages by the robot icon that appears when you run your mouse over the component.

How FrontPage
Components Work

In essence, FrontPage Components provide special instructions to the web server software—instructions that go beyond those typically included as part of the standard HTML instructions that comprise a standard web page. Not every web server understands these special instructions, however. FrontPage-generated FrontPage Components only work on web servers that have either the FrontPage Personal Web Server installed (as might be the case in a small intranet) or FrontPage Server Extensions installed (as might be the case on a large intranet or on an Internet server.)

These special instructions created by the FrontPage Component are called SmartHTML. For example, when you include the Hit Counter in your web page, the following SmartHTML code is generated:

If a web page with this SmartHTML code is displayed by a web server that can correctly interpret the code—say a web server with FrontPage Server Extensions—the web server returns a standard HTML page but substitutes the number of hits in place of the SmartHTML.

```
<p><!--webbot bot="HitCounter" startspan i-image="0" i-digits="0" i-resetvalue="0"
u-custom b-reset="FALSE" preview="&lt;strong&gt;Hit Counter&lt;/strong&gt;" --><strong>Hit
bot="HitCounter" i-checksum="12089" endspan --></p>
```

Annotating Web Pages with Comments

If you need to write notes to yourself and you don't want these notes to clutter your web page or to be viewed by web page visitors, you can add Comment Components.

TIP

Comments aren't part of the actual HTML document that will be viewed on the web. They only appear when you view the document using FrontPage Editor.

TIP

To edit a Comment, double-click the comment and add your changes in the Comment dialog box. To delete a Comment, select the comment text and press the Delete key.

Insert a Comment

1 Click in your web page to place the insertion point where you want to insert a comment.

2 Click the Insert FrontPage Component toolbar button.

3 Select Comment from the list, and click OK.

4 Type the comment you want to add to the web page.

5 Click OK to place the comment at the insertion point location.

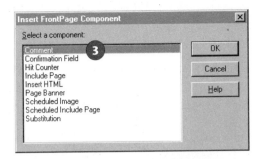

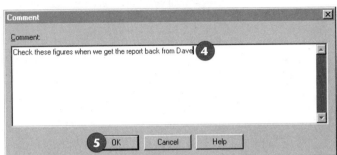

Confirming Visitor Input

You use Confirmation Fields on Confirmation Form Pages to verify the information a visitor has provided. In order for a Confirmation Field to work, you must have a form created for collecting information and a confirmation form attached to that form.

SEE ALSO

For more information about creating a Confirmation Form Page, see pages 187–188.

TIP

You must enter the form field name exactly as you have named it on the form. If you can't remember the field's name, right-click it, choose the shortcut menu's Form Field Properties command, and jot down the field's name.

Insert a Confirmation Field

1. Open the Confirmation Form web page to which you want to add the confirmation field.

2. Click to place the insertion point where you want to add the confirmation field, and click the Insert FrontPage Component toolbar button.

3. Select Confirmation Field from the list box, and click OK.

4. In the Confirmation Field Component Properties dialog box, enter the name of the form field you want to confirm and click OK.

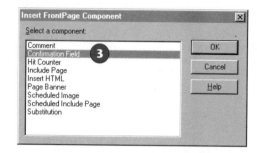

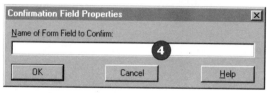

Inserting Hit Counters

Hit Counters are a very popular feature of many web pages. They let both web site visitors and web site creators easily see how much traffic a web page is getting.

 Visitors

Insert a Hit Counter

1 Open the web page in which you want to place the Hit Counter (most likely the Home page of your web).

2 Click to place the insertion point where you want to add the Hit Counter, and click the Insert FrontPage Component toolbar button.

3 Select Hit Counter from the list box, and click OK.

4 Select a look for the Hit Counter by clicking one of the Counter Style option buttons.

5 Check the Fixed Number Of Digits box if you want to fix your counter size at a certain number of digits.

6 Click OK.

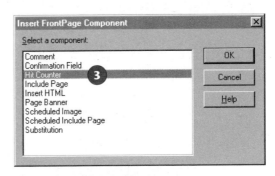

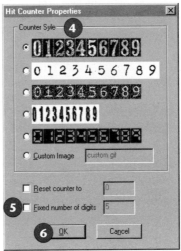

9

Inserting Include Page Components

To simplify the tasks of maintaining your web site and keeping it up to date, you may want FrontPage to change some of the information on your web pages automatically. The Include Page Component serves this purpose by inserting the web page you specify at the location you select.

TIP

Using the Include Page Component. *You can use the Include Page Component when you have several web pages that require identical text, graphic images, or formatting. The Include Page Component is similar to header or footers used in word processing. When the web page named by the Include Page Component changes, so do all the pages that use the Include Page Component.*

Insert the Include Component

1 Open the web page in which you want to place the Include Page Component.

2 Click the Insert FrontPage Component toolbar button.

3 Select Include Page from the list box, and click OK.

4 Type the URL address for the web page you want to include, or click the Browse button to browse the current web for the page.

5 Click OK.

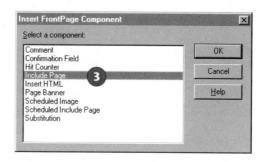

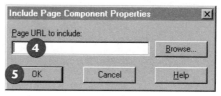

Inserting HTML

Although you can insert HTML instructions directly on the HTML tab in FrontPage Editor, you can also insert HTML Markup as a FrontPage Component. By inserting it as a FrontPage component, FrontPage does not edit it or attempt to display it on the Normal tab.

Insert the HTML Component

1 Open the web page in which you want to place the HTML.

2 Click the Insert FrontPage Component toolbar button.

3 Select Insert HTML from the list box, and click OK.

4 Type the HTML instructions in the HTML Markup dialog box.

5 Click OK.

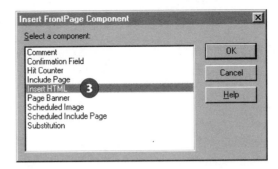

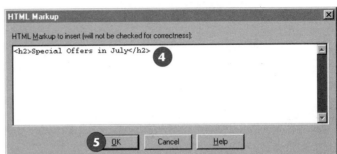

Inserting Page Banners

A Page Banner runs across the top of each page in a web site and identifies the page.

TIP

If the web page does not use a theme, clicking the Image option button is the same as clicking Text.

TIP

If the web page uses a theme, clicking the Text option button displays the web page title in the theme's font but without the banner image.

Insert a Page Banner

1 Open the web page in which you want to place the Page Banner.

2 Click the Insert FrontPage Component toolbar button.

3 Select Page Banner from the list box, and click OK.

4 Click the Image option button to create a banner using the font and banner image from the current theme. Or click the Text option button to create a banner displaying only the page title.

5 Click OK.

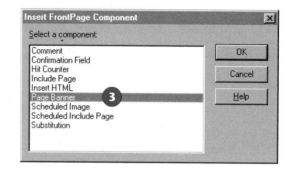

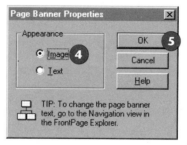

Inserting Scheduled Images

You use Scheduled Images when you want to display particular images for a specific amount of time, for example, for selected months or seasons. You might also use Scheduled Images to illustrate sales promotions or limited-time offers.

TIP

Editing a Scheduled Image. *You can't add a border or change the image type or alignment of a Scheduled Image. However, you can link or unlink the image using the Edit menu's Hyperlink or Unlink command.*

TIP

If the Scheduled Image expiration date passes and you have not supplied an optional image, the Expired Scheduled Image message appears in place of the image.

Insert a Scheduled Image

1 Open the web page in which you want to place the Scheduled Image.

2 Click the Insert FrontPage Component toolbar button.

3 Select Scheduled Image from the Select A Component list box, and click OK.

4 Type the name of the image you want to include in the web page using the Image To Include text box. Or click the Browse button to display the Current Web dialog box, and select an image from the list box.

5 Type the date the image should start appearing in the web page.

6 Type the date the image should stop appearing in the web page.

7 Supply an optional image that should appear before or after the original image appears.

8 Click OK.

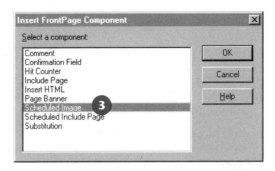

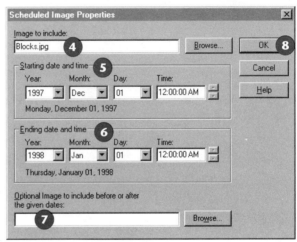

Inserting Scheduled Include Pages

Just as you would use Scheduled Images to display images for a specific amount of time, you use the Scheduled Include Page Components to display an entire page of content for a specific amount of time. For example, you would use a Scheduled Include Page if you wanted to regularly update a web site by substituting new web pages. With Scheduled Include Pages, the links automatically change when the time period expires and you only have to work with the individual pages of included content.

Insert the Scheduled Include Page Component

1 Open the web page in which you want to place the Scheduled Include Page Component.

2 Click the Insert FrontPage Component toolbar button.

3 Select Scheduled Include Page from the list box, and click OK.

4 Type the URL for the web page you want to include.

5 Type the date the web page should start appearing.

6 Type the date the web page should stop appearing.

7 Optionally, supply the URL for another web page that should appear before or after the scheduled web page appears.

8 Click OK.

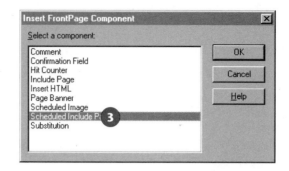

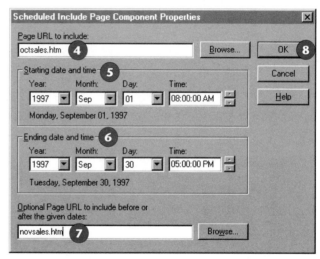

Inserting Substitution Components

You use Substitution Components to display configuration variables on a web page. Configuration variables include such bits of information as the web site author, a page's description, the name of the person who last modified the web site page, and other user-defined configuration variables.

SEE ALSO

For more information about creating and editing configuration variables, see pages 194–195.

TIP

Making a Substitution Component work. *In order for the Substitution Component to work, you must supply values for each of the variables listed in the Substitute With drop-down list box. To do this, start Microsoft FrontPage Explorer, choose the Tools menu's Web Settings command, click the Add button on the Parameters tab, and then supply the values.*

Insert the Substitution Component

1 Open the web page in which you want to place the Substitution Component.

2 Click the Insert FrontPage Component toolbar button.

3 Select Substitution from the list box, and click OK.

4 Select a substitution variable from the Substitute With drop-down list box.

5 Click OK.

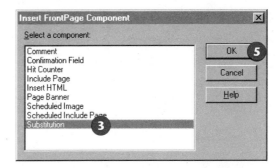

9

Working with FrontPage Components

A few tasks apply to all of the FrontPage Components you can create. For example, you can access the FrontPage Component's Properties dialog box in the same manner. All FrontPage Components also create HTML code, which you can view and edit as you would the rest of the HTML code on a web page. You can also delete FrontPage Components in exactly the same way.

> **TIP**
>
> *To restore a deleted FrontPage Component, click the Undo toolbar button.*

Change the Properties of a FrontPage Component Field

1 Open the web page with the FrontPage Component.

2 Double-click the FrontPage Component.

3 Use the Properties dialog box FrontPage displays to make your changes, and click OK when you're finished.

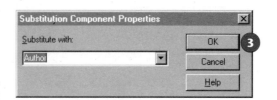

View the HTML Code Created by a FrontPage Component

1 Open the web page with the FrontPage Component.

2 Click the HTML tab in FrontPage Editor.

3 Click the Normal tab to resume editing the web page.

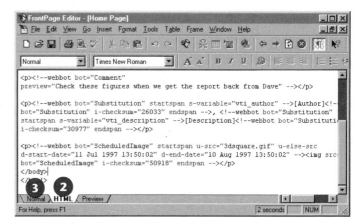

Delete a FrontPage Component

1 Open the web page with the FrontPage Component you want to delete.

2 Select the component you want to delete by clicking it.

3 Press the Delete key.

Inserting Timestamps

A timestamp inserts the date and oftentimes also the time of day a page was last edited and saved or the last time it was automatically updated (as a part of recalculating hyperlinks, for instance). Web site visitors can use the timestamp to tell how current the information is.

Insert a Timestamp

1 Open the web page where you want a timestamp.

2 Choose the Insert menu's Timestamp command.

3 Click one of the Display option buttons to tell FrontPage whether you want the timestamp to show the last time the web page was edited or the last time it was automatically updated.

4 Select a date format from the Date Format drop-down list box.

5 Select a time format from the Time Format drop-down list box.

6 Click OK.

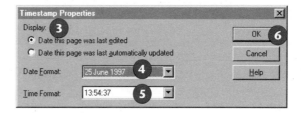

9

Inserting a Table of Contents

A table of contents creates an outline of hyperlinks to each page in your web site. Visitors to your web site can use the table of contents to navigate through the web site. The table of contents can also be configured so that it updates itself whenever you add, delete, or rename a page.

TIP

If you want a list of all the web pages in your web site, assign your Home page as the starting point for the table of contents.

TIP

Manual recompute. *Very large web sites will take a long time to recompute when the Recompute Table Of Contents box is checked. If you don't select this option and you want to recompute the table of contents manually, open the page with the table of contents and then save the page.*

TRY THIS

Click the Preview tab to see the computed table of contents.

Insert a Table of Contents

1. Open the web page in which you want to place the table of contents.

2. Choose the Insert menu's Table Of Contents command.

3. Type the URL for the first web page you want included in the table of contents. Or click the Browse button and select a web page from the dialog box FrontPage Editor displays.

4. Select a heading size from the Heading Size drop-down list box.

5. Check the Show Each Page Only Once box to list a web page only once in the table of contents.

6. Check the Show Pages With No Incoming Hyperlinks box to display all pages on the site—including those that aren't referenced, or linked, to other pages.

7. Check the Recompute Table Of Contents When Any Other Page Is Edited box to ensure that any changes you make to the web site—such as adding a new page—are reflected in an updated table of contents.

8. Click OK.

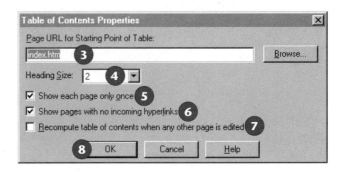

Inserting Navigation Bars

Many of FrontPage's web wizards come with a navigation bar, or a row of buttons that link to the main pages in a web site. You can, however, also create your own navigation bar so that visitors to your web site have quick and easy links to the pages you consider most important.

[Home] [Feedback] [Contents] [Search]

TRY THIS

To add a shared navigation bar to all web pages in a web site, open the web site in FrontPage Explorer and choose the Tools menu's Shared Borders command.

Insert a Navigation Bar

1 Open the web page in which you want to place the navigation bar.

2 Choose the Insert menu's Navigation Bar command.

3 Specify which pages you want included as hyperlinks in the navigation bar.

4 Specify whether you want the navigation bar to run horizontally or vertically across the page and whether you want text or button links to pages.

5 Click OK.

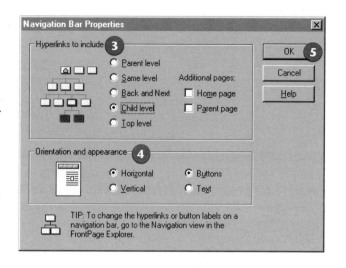

9

10

Working with Forms

Forms let you collect information from site visitors. To use a form, a visitor simply types information in the form's fields, clicks a button that submits the information to the web site server, and then the server collects and processes the information according to the instructions of the form's handler.

All Microsoft FrontPage forms have several basic elements:

◆ Questions or requests for information

◆ Fields in which visitors type information

◆ Submit and Reset buttons that let the visitor control whether he or she submits or clears the form

◆ Form handlers associated with the form that control what happens to the visitor's input

It's important to note that FrontPage doesn't require you to create computer programming scripts in order to use forms or handle the form data. (This is the usual case when including forms in a web site.) FrontPage creates the scripts that handle the forms automatically.

Creating Forms from Templates

You create feedback and user registration forms to gather various types of information from visitors. Use a feedback form to collect feedback about your site, services, or products. Use a user registration form so that visitors can register themselves to access a web site.

Make up a username:

Make up a password:

SEE ALSO

For information about editing form fields, see pages 174–185 later in this section.

Create a Feedback Form

1 Start FrontPage Editor.

2 Choose the File menu's New command.

3 Select Feedback Form from the list box.

4 Click OK.

5 Customize the text, comments, or fields of the form.

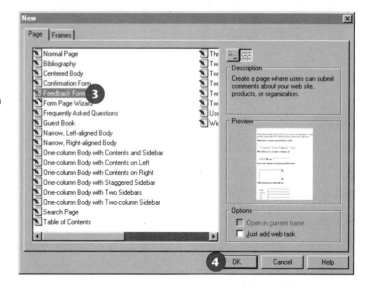

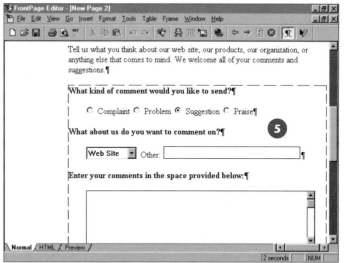

Create a User Registration Page

1 Start FrontPage Editor.

2 Choose the File menu's New command.

3 Select User Registration from the list box.

4 Click OK.

5 Customize the text, comments, and fields of the form.

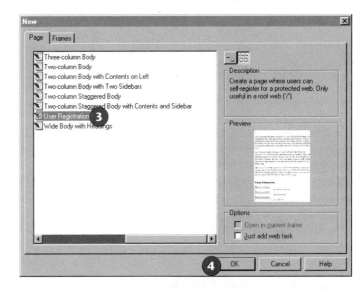

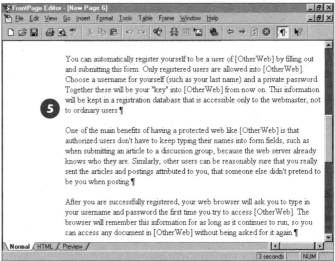

Using the Form Page Wizard

The Form Page Wizard speeds up the creation of forms and provides form templates for certain types of forms you might want to use again and again. The wizard not only creates a form for you but also attaches the proper form handler to the form.

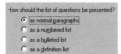

Create a Form Using the Form Page Wizard

1 Start Microsoft FrontPage Editor.

2 Choose the File menu's New command, and then select Form Page Wizard from the list box. Click OK, and then click Next.

3 Type the URL in the Page URL text box, type the title in the Page Title text box, and then click Next.

4 Click the Add button.

5 Select the type of information you'll collect with this form from the list box.

6 Edit the way you want the question asked, and then click Next twice.

7 Set the options for the question you selected, give the variable a name, and then click Next twice.

8 Describe how your questions should be presented by clicking the appropriate option buttons, and then click Next.

9 Describe how the information you collect with a form should be handled by clicking the appropriate option buttons.

10 Click Finish.

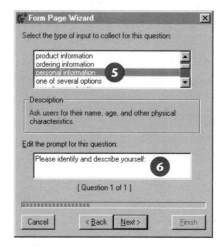

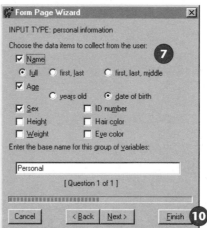

The Parts of a Form

You can use a variety of buttons and boxes on the forms that you create.

Text box

Use a text box when you want to collect specific pieces of information from web site visitors, such as their names, addresses, or e-mail aliases.

Scrolling text box

Use a scrolling text box when you can't estimate how much room visitors will need or what structure or form visitors will use for entering information.

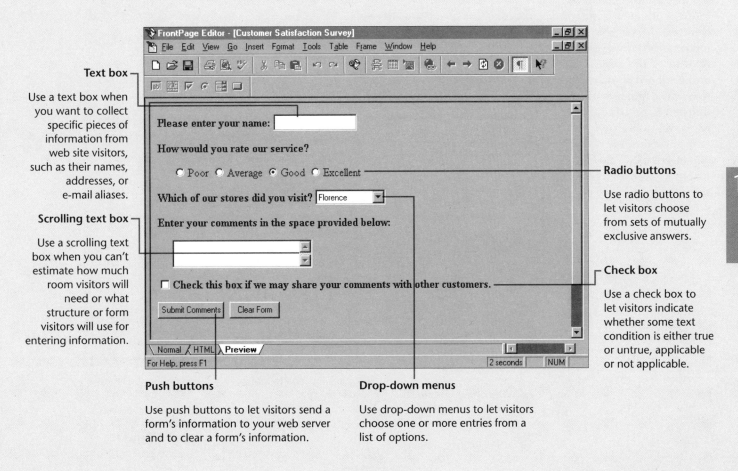

Radio buttons

Use radio buttons to let visitors choose from sets of mutually exclusive answers.

Check box

Use a check box to let visitors indicate whether some text condition is either true or untrue, applicable or not applicable.

Push buttons

Use push buttons to let visitors send a form's information to your web server and to clear a form's information.

Drop-down menus

Use drop-down menus to let visitors choose one or more entries from a list of options.

Inserting One-Line Text Boxes

FrontPage provides a variety of methods to create new forms or add new form elements to a page. Which method you choose depends on what you're already doing and what you want to do next. You use one-line text boxes to collect responses to short-answer type questions. For example, you might use a one-line text box to ask for a person's name, address, or telephone number.

Insert a One-Line Text Box Field

1. Open the web page in which you want to place the One-Line Text Box field.

2. Click the One-Line Text Box button on the Forms toolbar.

3. Click to place the insertion point to the left of the One-Line Text Box field.

4. Type the title for the One-Line Text Box field.

Constrain One-Line Text Box Field Responses

1. Right-click the One-Line Text Box field.

2. Choose the shortcut menu's Form Field Validation command.

3. Optionally, constrain the allowable response content to text, integers, or numbers only.

4. Define the constraint using the Text Format boxes and Numeric Format buttons.

5. Optionally, constrain the response length.

6. Optionally, describe the range of acceptable answers.

7. Click OK.

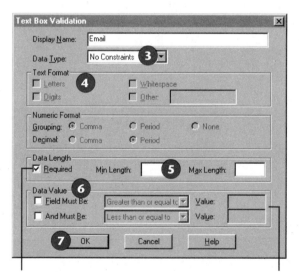

Check this box to require a response in the One-Line Text Box field.

Describe the range of values numerically for numeric responses or alphabetically for textual responses.

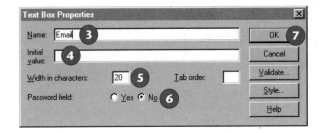

Change the Properties of a One-Line Text Box Field

1 Right-click the One-Line Text Box field.

2 Choose the shortcut menu's Form Field Properties command.

3 Type the name of the field in the Name text box.

4 Optionally, type the initial value to be placed inside the One-Line Text Box field in the Initial Value text box.

5 Optionally, change the width of the field in the Width In Characters box.

6 Optionally, click a Password Field option button.

7 Click OK.

Inserting Scrolling Text Boxes

Scrolling text boxes work much like one-line text boxes except they allow web site visitors to enter more information. If you choose not to constrain the length of visitors' inputs in scrolling text boxes, they can type up to numerous paragraphs.

TIP

As a general rule, you'll want to keep your forms short. Web visitors typically don't and won't spend more than a few minutes filling out an online form.

TIP

A scrolling text box is best used for visitors to enter comments or special requests for information.

Insert a Scrolling Text Box Field

1 Open the web page in which you want to place the Scrolling Text Box field.

2 Click the Scrolling Text Box button on the Forms toolbar.

3 Click to place the insertion point to the left of the Scrolling Text Box field.

4 Type the title for the Scrolling Text Box field.

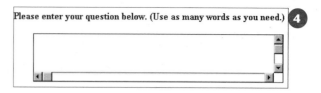

Change the Properties of a Scrolling Text Box Field

1 Right-click the Scrolling Text Box field.

2 Choose the shortcut menu's Form Field Properties command.

3 Type the name of the field in the Name text box.

4 Optionally, type the initial value to be placed inside the Scrolling Text Box field in the Initial Value text box.

5 Optionally, change the width of the field in the Width In Characters box.

6 Optionally, change the height of the field in the Number Of Lines box.

7 Click OK.

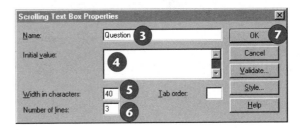

10

Inserting Check Boxes and Radio Buttons

Most forms include at least a few radio buttons (also called option buttons) or check boxes. Radio buttons are like the bubbles on tests that you darken with a #2 pencil. You use radio buttons with multiple-choice type answers where the choices are typically mutually exclusive. You might, for instance, use a set of radio buttons to ask which age range a visitor fits into. You use check boxes to ask visitors to mark all options that apply. You might, for instance, use check boxes to allow visitors to request information or order products.

TIP

Check boxes allow the visitor to check all options that apply. Radio buttons are used for selecting one option from a group of options.

Insert a Check Box Field

1. Open the web page in which you want to place the Check Box field.

2. Click the Check Box button on the Forms toolbar.

3. Click to place the insertion point to the right of the Check Box field.

4. Type the title for the Check Box field.

☐ **Please send me a catalog.** ④

Insert a Radio Button Field

1. Open the web page in which you want to place the Radio Button field.

2. Click the Radio Button button on the Forms toolbar.

3. Click to place the insertion point to the right of the Radio Button field.

4. Type the title for the Radio Button field.

How would you rank your level of experience?

○ Beginning ● Intermediate ○ Advanced ○ Expert ④

Name a Radio Button or Check Box Field

1 Right-click the Radio Button or Check Box field.

2 Choose the shortcut menu's Form Field Properties command.

3 Type the name of the field in the Name text box.

4 Click OK.

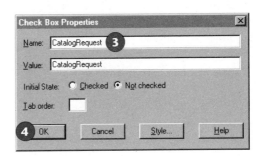

TIP

Use the Display Name text box to tell FrontPage how to name the form field if it must display a message box alerting a visitor that he or she did not properly enter information in the field as required by the field's validation properties.

Require a Response to a Radio Button Field

1 Right-click the Radio Button field.

2 Choose the shortcut menu's Form Field Validation command.

3 Check the Data Required box to require a response to the set of radio buttons.

4 Click OK.

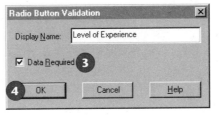

10

Inserting Drop-Down Menu Fields

You use the Drop-Down Menu button on the Forms toolbar to create drop-down menus and list boxes for your forms. Drop-down menus and list boxes give web site visitors the opportunity to scroll through a list of possible responses and then pick the best answer or even several answers, depending on how you set up the fields. Drop-down menus work in a fashion similar to radio buttons, but they take up less room on the screen, making them more appropriate for long, detailed lists of options.

TIP

A drop-down menu offers a visitor the option to select multiple items from a list.

Insert a Drop-Down Menu Field

1 Open the web page in which you want to place the Drop-Down Menu field.

2 Click the Drop-Down Menu button on the Forms toolbar.

3 Place the insertion point to the right of the Drop-Down Menu field.

4 Type the name of the Drop-Down Menu field.

Constrain Drop-Down Menu Field Responses

1 Right-click the Drop-Down Menu field.

2 Choose the shortcut menu's Form Field Validation command.

3 Check the Data Required box if you want to require a response to the Drop-Down Menu field.

4 If you want to allow multiple answers to the field, enter the minimum and maximum number of allowable responses.

5 Check the Disallow First Item box if you want to use the first item as a line for providing instructions (such as "Please pick one of the following").

6 Click OK.

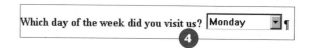

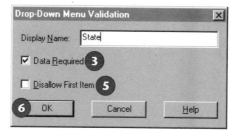

TIP

TIP

By default, the value for the drop-down menu choice is the same as the choice name. If you want to change the value, check the Specify Value box. Note that what you type in the Choice text box is still what the viewer will see in the drop-down menu.

TIP

By entering a value greater than 1 in the Height text box, you create a list box.

Add Choices to a Drop-Down Menu Field

1 Right-click the Drop-Down Menu field.

2 Choose the shortcut menu's Form Field Properties command.

3 Type the name of the field in the Name text box.

4 Click the Add button.

5 Type the name of the first item to be listed in the Drop-Down Menu List field in the Choice text box.

6 Click the Initial State option button as Selected if you want the choice selected in the form.

7 Click OK.

8 Repeat steps 4 through 7 for each additional item you want to add to the drop-down menu.

9 Click OK.

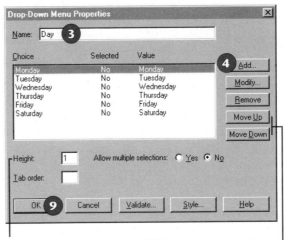

Change the number of drop-down menu choices shown using the Height box.

Click the Move Up or Move Down buttons to move the choice up or down in the drop-down menu.

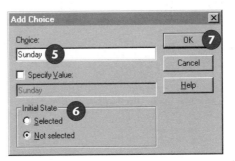

10

Inserting Push Buttons

In order for a form to function, visitors must have some way of submitting the form so that the responses can be gathered and processed by the form's handler. In this sense, push buttons play one of the most important roles in a form: they are the buttons that visitors use to tell the form handlers "Go!" When you insert these buttons in your forms, therefore, you need to make them visible and identifiable.

TIP

The Submit Button field's label can be changed to any Value/ Label you choose. Supply a new Value/Label to customize your form.

Insert a Push Button Field

1 Open the web page in which you want to place the Push Button field.

2 Click the Push Button button on the Forms toolbar.

FrontPage inserts Submit and Reset push buttons by default when you insert a form field other than a Push Button field.

What push buttons do.
*Clicking a Submit button tells
the web browser to send the
form's information to the web
server. All forms need a Submit
button of some sort. Clicking a
Reset button tells the web
browser to reset the form's
buttons and boxes to their
initial, or default, values.
Clicking a Normal button tells
the web browser to run the
script, or program, you attach to
the button.*

Describing a Push Button Field

1 Right-click the Push Button field.

2 Choose the shortcut menu's Form Field Properties command.

3 Type the name of the field in the Name text box.

4 Change the Value/Label of the Push Button field.

5 Optionally, change the type of button by clicking the Normal, Submit, or Reset option buttons.

6 Click OK.

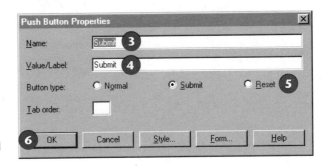

10

Inserting Image Fields

To make your forms more interesting, you can also use images as form fields. For example, instead of using a text list to describe the products visitors can order over your web site, you can display a thumbnail graphic of each one. By doing so, you not only make your form more visually appealing but you also make it more informative. Visitors unfamiliar with your products can see exactly what you're offering before they place their orders.

TIP

You cannot insert an Image field using the Forms toolbar.

Insert an Image Field

1 Open the web page in which you want to place the Image field.

2 Choose the Insert menu's Form Field command.

3 Choose the Form Field submenu's Image command.

4 Select an image from the list box or click the Clip Art button to use a clip art image.

5 Click OK.

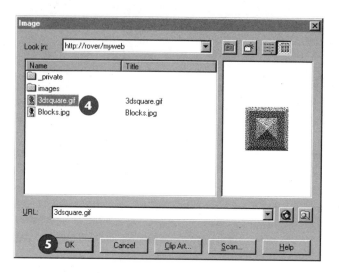

TIP

To insert a label beside a form field, insert the form field and type the text you want to use as a label beside it. Then choose the Insert menu's Form Field command and the Form Field submenu's Label command.

TIP

The tools on the Image toolbar do not work with Image Form fields.

SEE ALSO

To add an image to be used as a hyperlink, see pages 74–75.

Change the Properties of an Image Field

1 Right-click the Image field.

2 Choose the shortcut menu's Form Field Properties command.

3 Type the name of the field in the Name text box.

4 Optionally, click the Image Properties button.

5 Click the General tab.

6 Optionally, change the Image type by clicking the GIF or JPEG option buttons.

7 Optionally, enter alternative representations in the Low-Res and Text text boxes.

8 Click OK to return to the Image Form Field Properties dialog box.

9 Click OK.

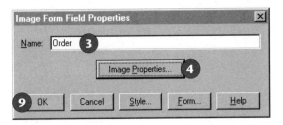

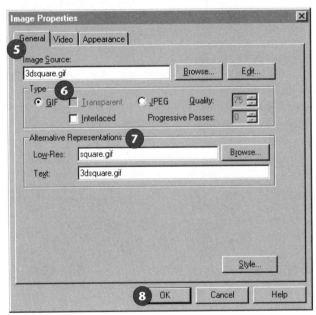

10

Saving Form Results

Once you have your form created, you need to specify what you want to do with the data the form collects. For Survey and Feedback forms, you use the Save Results form handler to tell the server what information you want to collect from visitors and how you want this information stored.

> **TIP**
>
> **About form handlers.** *A form handler is simply a program that runs on a web server. The form handler program runs whenever someone submits a form to it. The most common forms run the Save Results form handler.*

> **TIP**
>
> **Testing a form.** *You'll want to test your form before placing it in your web site. Specifically, you want to verify that together the form and the form handler do whatever you want them to do—such as correctly collecting and storing the form information.*

Set up a File for Form Results

1 Open the web page with the form.

2 Right-click the form area.

3 Choose the shortcut menu's Form Properties command.

4 Click the Send To option button.

5 Enter the name of the file where you want to save the information that web site visitors enter in the form.

6 Optionally, if you want the form results sent to an e-mail address, enter the e-mail address.

7 Click the Options button.

8 Select the file format from the File Format drop-down list box.

9 Optionally, check the Include Field Names box.

10 Optionally, click the Saved Fields tab and use the Additional Information To Save check boxes to collect and save additional information about your web site visitors.

11 Click OK.

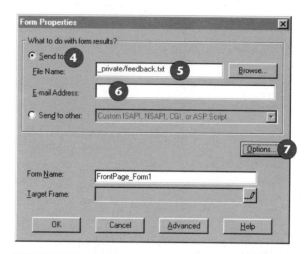

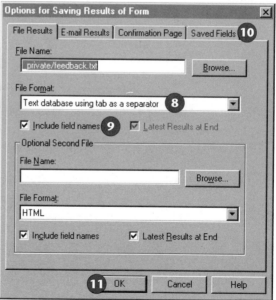

Creating a Confirmation Form Page

Use a Confirmation form to acknowledge a web visitor's input on a Feedback, Survey, or User Registration form. The form's fields redisplay the user's input so that he or she can edit any information incorrectly entered.

> **E-mail:** [UserEmail]
> **Telephone:** [UserTel]
> **FAX:** [UserFAX]

TIP

After you create an interactive web page, you customize the web page by editing the individual fields. See Section 9 for more information on how to add, edit, and remove individual FrontPage Components.

TIP

If you rename a field on one form, be sure to also rename the field on other forms. If you don't, those other forms' fields won't show the right information.

Create a Confirmation Form Page

1 Start FrontPage Editor.

2 Choose the File menu's New command.

3 Select Confirmation Form from the list box.

4 Click OK.

5 Customize the form fields by right-clicking them and choosing FrontPage Component Properties from the shortcut menu.

6 Enter a new field name to confirm.

7 Click OK.

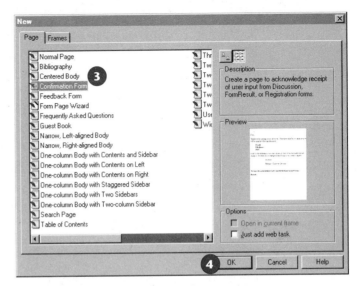

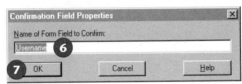

Attaching a Confirmation Form

Once you have a Confirmation form created, you can attach it to a form (for instance a Survey or Feedback form) so that it appears whenever a visitor completes the form.

SEE ALSO

For more information about inserting Confirmation Components, see page 156.

Attach a Confirmation Form to a Form Page

1 Open the form page to which you want to attach the Confirmation form.

2 Right-click the form.

3 Choose the shortcut menu's Form Properties command.

4 Click the Options button.

5 Click the Confirmation Page tab.

6 Specify the Confirmation form you want displayed after the form page has been completed in the URL Of Confirmation Page text box. Or click the Browse button to locate the Confirmation form.

7 Click OK.

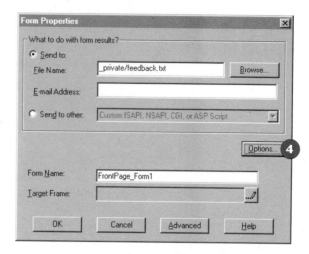

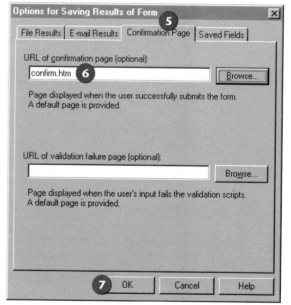

Setting Up a Second Save Results File

If you want the information you collect on a form stored in two different places, you need to set up a second Save Results file associated with the Save Results form handler. You might want to do this, for instance, if you want to post the results of a survey on a web page and save them in a file as well.

Set Up a Second Save Results File

1 Open the form page.

2 Right-click the form area.

3 Choose the shortcut menu's Form Properties command.

4 Click the Options button.

5 Type the name of the second Save Results page or file in the Optional Second File's File Name text box.

6 Select the file format from the File Format drop-down list box.

7 Click OK.

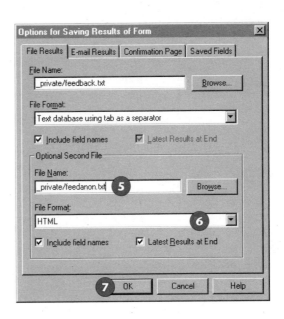

Restricting Web Access to Registered Users

If you create a User Registration page to allow only registered users to access a web site, visitors must supply a name and password in order to view the site. The Registration form handler handles the list of registered users and displays the form requiring visitors to enter a name and password.

Form Submission

Make up a username:
-- you can use mixed case
Make up a password:
-- keep this private!

TIP

You can constrain the list of allowable responses to the User Registration form's fields. For information on how to do this, see page 174.

Set Up a List of Registered Users and Passwords

1 Open the User Registration page.

2 Right-click the form area.

3 Choose the shortcut menu's Form Properties command.

4 Click the Options button.

5 Optionally, change the name of the web in the FrontPage Web Name text box.

6 Optionally, change the name of the User Name field in the User Name Fields text box.

7 Optionally, change the name of the Password field in the Password Field text box.

8 Optionally, change the name of the Password-Verify field in the Password Confirmation Field text box.

9 Optionally, change the URL of the web page you want to display when a visitor fails to register successfully in the URL Of Registration Failure Page text box.

10 Click OK.

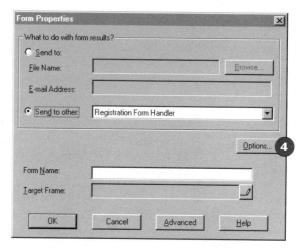

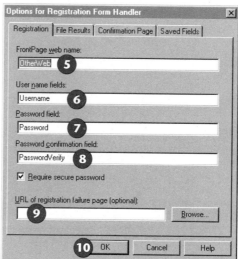

TIP

You can also change the Registration form's Confirmation URL by clicking the Confirmation tab and specifying the web page or form you want displayed after the Registration form has been completed. For more information on attaching Confirmation forms, see page 188.

Change Registration Form Results

1 Open the User Registration page.

2 Right-click the form area.

3 Choose the shortcut menu's Form Properties command.

4 Click the Options button.

5 Click the File Results tab.

6 Optionally, change the file used to store registration information in the File Name text box.

7 Optionally, select a file format for the results file from the File Format drop-down list box.

8 Optionally, click the Saved Fields tab and use the Additional Information To Save check boxes to save the time, date, remote computer name, user name, or browser type to the results file.

9 Click OK.

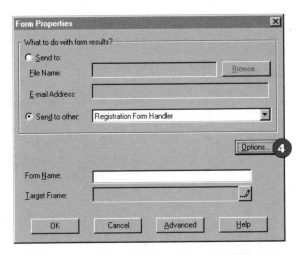

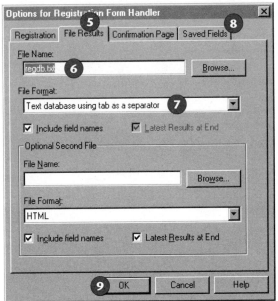

Administering a Web Site

The work of administering a large Internet web site often exceeds the burden that many web publishers will want to bear. Nevertheless, you should not assume that web site administration is out of reach or impractical if you are new to web publishing. Microsoft FrontPage provides numerous tools for making web site administration relatively easy for small web sites.

For example, you can make several changes to the web site's appearance and operation. You can easily change the number, type, and settings of the configuration variables that FrontPage's web wizards create and that the Substitution Components use. (A configuration variable is just a piece of information about a web site or web page that can be displayed by a Substitution Component.) And you can easily change or update the web site title and name.

Working with your web site's security is more involved, but it's still very straightforward to fine-tune your web site's security settings. For example, you can specify which users can browse, or visit, a web site. You can identify which users and groups of users can make changes to a web site's pages and graphic images. And you can even specify which computers people can use to browse a web site.

Note, too, that the work of actually publishing a web site to a web server is quite simple. All you do is choose a command and then answer a few questions. (FrontPage publishes web sites both to servers that use FrontPage Server Extensions and to those that don't.)

Working with Configuration Variables

Microsoft FrontPage Explorer uses configuration variables to supply Substitution Components with commonly used pieces of information you find in a web site: your company name, an e-mail address, and so forth. While you typically create and set these configuration variables as part of running the wizard that creates a web site, you can make changes to the variables later.

SEE ALSO

For more information about working with Substitution Components, refer to page 163.

Add a Configuration Variable

1 Choose the Tools menu's Web Settings command in FrontPage Explorer.

2 Click the Parameters tab.

3 Click the Add button.

4 Type a name for the configuration variable in the Name text box.

5 Type the value for the configuration variable in the Value list box.

6 Click OK.

7 Click OK.

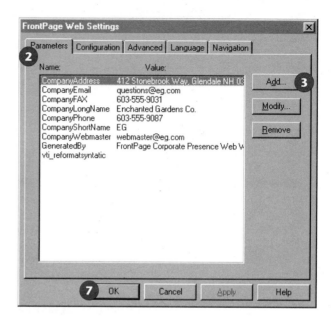

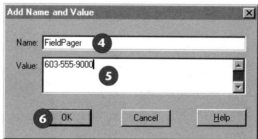

Change a Configuration Variable

1 Choose the Tools menu's Web Settings command.

2 Click the Parameters tab.

3 Select the configuration variable you want to change by clicking it.

4 Click the Modify button.

5 Type the value for the configuration variable in the Value box.

6 Click OK.

7 Click OK.

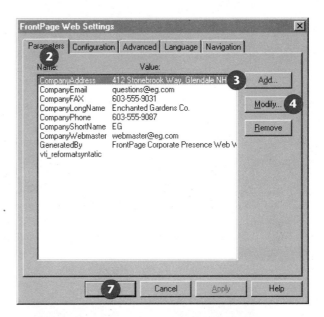

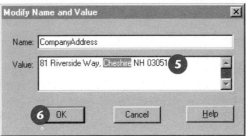

Changing Web Site Settings

When you create a web site, you give the web site a name that the web server as well as FrontPage will use to refer to the site. You also, indirectly, set the web site's language and choose the web site's characters. You can change these web site settings later by using the Tools menu's Web Settings command.

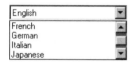

TIP

You can click the Apply button if you want to make a change using the FrontPage Web Settings dialog box—such as changing the language—without closing the dialog box.

Change the Web Site Name and Title

1. Choose the Tools menu's Web Settings command.

2. Click the Configuration tab.

3. Type the name for the web site in the Web Name text box.

4. Type the title for the web site in the Web Title text box.

5. Click OK.

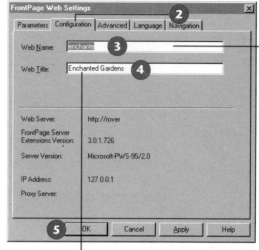

The name FrontPage uses for the directory holding the site's web pages and images. Whatever you enter here must be a valid directory name on the site's web server.

The name FrontPage uses to refer to the web site.

Change the Web Site's Language

1. Choose the Tools menu's Web Settings command.

2. Click the Language tab.

3. Activate the Default Web Language drop-down list box; then select the language you want the web site to use.

4. Activate the Default HTML Encoding drop-down list box; then select the default HTML coding style you want to use.

5. Click OK.

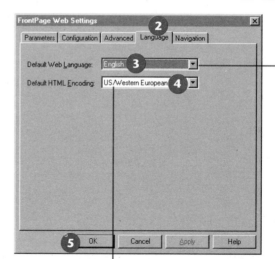

The language you choose with this setting determines which language FrontPage Server Extensions uses to send messages to web site visitors.

The Default HTML Encoding selection you make determines which default character FrontPage Explorer will use for any new web pages you create.

Working with Web Site Security

You can control access to your web site in a variety of ways. For example, you can specify who can make changes to the web site (such as adding or editing pages) and who can browse your web site. You can also specify which computers people can use to browse your web site.

○ Use same permissions
⦿ Use unique permissions

TIP

If the current web is the root web on the server, the Permissions dialog box does not have a Settings tab. The web already has unique permissions.

TIP

Some web servers do not allow you to set user permissions.

Use Unique Permissions for a Web Site

1 Choose the Tools menu's Permissions command.

2 Click the Settings tab.

3 Click the Use Unique Permissions For This Web option button.

4 Click OK.

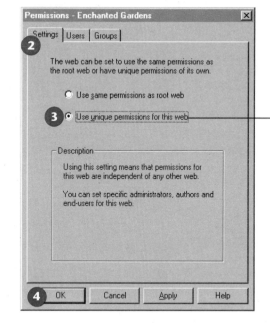

You indicate that you want to use unique permissions for a web site when you want to specify who can browse a web site and who can make changes to the web site.

Adding and Removing Users from a Web Site

After you have specified that you want to use unique permissions for web site users, you need to build a list of users and designate the permissions for each user. You might on occasion also want to remove a user from the list to deny him or her access to browse the web site.

TIP

To change the web site permissions, you must have administrator rights.

TIP

To specify a new user for a web site, you must first indicate that you want to use a unique set of permissions for the web site.

TIP

You can click the Apply button if you want to make a change using the Permissions dialog box—such as adding a new user—without closing the dialog box.

Specify a New User for a Web Site

1 Choose the Tools menu's Permissions command.

2 Click the Users tab.

3 Click the Add button.

4 Select the domain from the Obtain List From drop-down list box.

5 Select the new user's name from the Names list box, or enter a name for a new user.

6 Click the Add button.

7 Select a User Can option to specify what this user can or can't do.

8 Click OK.

9 Click OK.

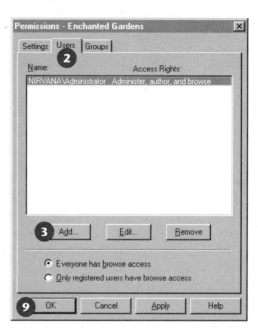

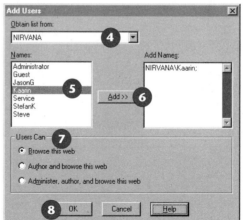

To remove a user from a web site, you must first indicate that you want to use a unique set of permissions for the web site.

You can click the Apply button if you want to make a change using the Permissions dialog box—such as removing a user—without closing the dialog box.

Remove a User from a Web Site

1 Choose the Tools menu's Permissions command.

2 Click the Users tab.

3 Select a user by clicking a name.

4 Click the Remove button.

5 Click OK.

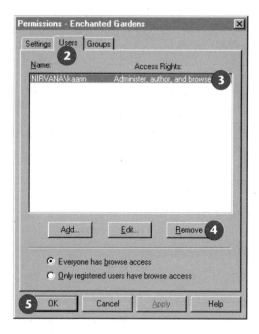

Specifying User Permissions

Once you have specified unique permissions for a web site, you can grant permissions for each individual user. You can give users varying levels of permission—from the ability to browse the web site only to the ability to author and administer the web site.

TIP

To specify who can browse a web site, you must first indicate that you want to use a unique set of permissions for the web site.

TIP

By default, users can access the web site from any computer. On some web servers, you can specify which computers people must use to administer, author, or browse a web site. Click the Computer tab, and set computer permissions using their IP addresses. Use the asterisk character as a wildcard to specify groups of computers that share certain digits.

Specify Who Can Browse a Web Site

1 Choose the Tools menu's Permissions command.

2 Click the Users tab.

3 Select an option to specify who can and who can't browse this web site.

4 Click OK.

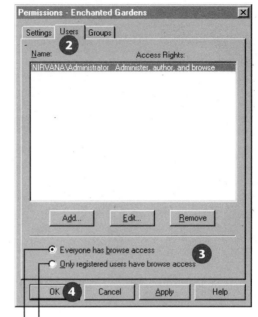

Select this option if you want only registered users to be able to browse the web site.

Select this option if you want everyone to be able to browse the web site.

Change an Existing User's Permissions for a Web Site

1. Choose the Tools menu's Permissions command.

2. Click the Users tab.

3. Select a user by clicking a name.

4. Click the Edit button.

5. Select a User Can option to specify what this user can or can't do.

6. Click OK.

7. Click OK.

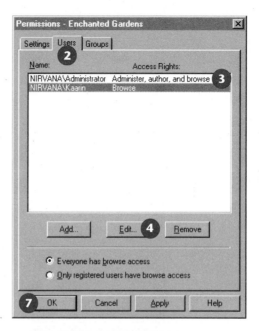

Adding and Removing User Groups from a Web Site

As with specifying individual user permissions for a web site, you can also specify permissions for a group of users. You do this by building a list of users to which you grant some level of access permission to the web site, and then you specify the level of permission for each group.

> **TIP**
>
> *Some web servers let you set permissions only for users or groups of users that are known to the server.*

Specify a New User Group for a Web Site

1 Choose the Tools menu's Permissions command.

2 Click the Groups tab.

3 Click the Add button.

4 Select the group from the Names list box, or enter a name for the group.

5 Click the Add button.

6 Click OK.

7 Click OK.

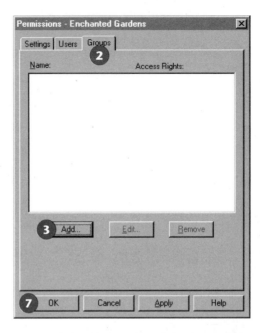

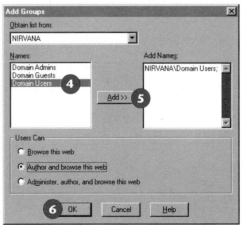

Remove a User Group from a Web Site

1. Choose the Tools menu's Permissions command.

2. Click the Groups tab.

3. Select a group from the list box.

4. Click the Remove button.

5. Click OK.

Changing Group Permissions

After you have compiled a list of user groups that you want to grant permission to browse your web site and have designated specific permissions for each group, you may at some point want to change a group's permission. Luckily, this is very easy to do.

TIP

To change an existing group's permissions for a web site, you must first indicate that you want to use a unique set of permissions for the web site.

Change an Existing User Group's Permissions for a Web Site

1 Choose the Tools menu's Permissions command.

2 Click the Groups tab.

3 Select a group from the list box.

4 Click the Edit button.

5 Click a User Can option button to specify what the users in this group can or can't do.

6 Click OK.

7 Click OK.

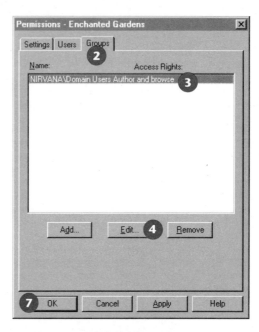

Publishing a Web Site

Once you finish creating a web site, you publish it to a web server so that people can visit the web site. In essence, when you publish a web site, you move all of a web site's pages and graphic images to a server. How you do this depends on whether or not the web server uses FrontPage Server Extensions.

TIP

If your web site includes FrontPage Components, the web server you use to publish your web site must have FrontPage Server Extensions installed.

TIP

If you publish your web site to a server that doesn't have FrontPage Server Extensions installed, FrontPage Explorer starts the Microsoft Web Publishing Wizard to publish your web site.

TIP

If you are publishing the root web, click the Include Child Webs option button to publish all webs within the root web.

Publish the Web Site to a Server

1 Click the Publish toolbar button.

2 Select the name of the web server to which you want to publish the web, or enter a new location directly in the text box.

3 Click OK.

4 If the web server asks for your name and password, enter them in the text boxes provided.

5 Click OK.

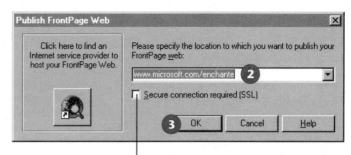

Check the Secure Connection Required box if you are publishing your web site on a server that supports Secure Sockets Layer (SSL) so that people can communicate with the server in a secure, encrypted manner, when transferring information such as credit card numbers.

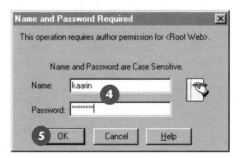

11

Deleting a Web Site

If you create a web site that you no longer use—perhaps the web site was merely one you used to learn FrontPage, for example—you can and should delete the web site. (You do this because web sites, particularly those that use many graphic images, require voluminous quantities of disk space.)

Drive C

TIP

You can't undelete a web site using the Microsoft Windows 95 or Windows NT Recycle Bin. For this reason, you'll want to make sure you really do want to delete a web site before choosing the Delete FrontPage Web command.

Delete a Web Site

1 Start FrontPage Explorer, and open the web site you want to delete.

2 Choose the File menu's Delete FrontPage Web command.

3 When FrontPage Explorer asks you to confirm your action, click Yes.

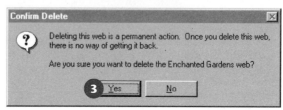

Index

Image Composer, 61
image fields, 184, 185
image maps. *See* hotspots
images. *See also* hotspots
  adding borders, 69
  adding hyperlinks, 74–75
  adding to table cells, 110–12
  adding to web pages, 60–61
  aligning, 68
  changing properties, 68–69
  commenting on, 29
  converting to GIF, 71
  converting to JPEG, 70
  copying between applications, 67
  copying between table cells, 112
  copying between web pages, 66
  copying to web pages, 60
  copying within web pages, 64, 65
  cropping, 63
  deleting from table cells, 113
  deleting from web sites, 28
  exporting, 31
  file formats, 60, 61, 70–71
  importing, 30
  low-resolution, 73
  making transparent, 68
  moving between table cells, 112
  moving within web pages, 64, 65
  resizing, 63, 110, 112
  rotating, 65
  saving, 96

images, *continued*
  Scheduled Image Component, 161
  as table background, 117
  as table cell background, 122
  text-only representations, 72
  tips for using, 62
  viewing list in FrontPage Explorer, 17–18
  viewing properties, 29
  as web page background, 136–38
importing
  images, 30
  web pages, 30
Include Page Component, 158
indenting paragraphs, 53
Internet. *See* World Wide Web
Internet protocols, 90
italicizing text, 48

Java applets
  banner ads, 151
  hover buttons, 150
JPEG file format, 60, 61, 70

left-aligning text, 52
line breaks, inserting, 52
lines
  coloring, 55
  customizing, 55
  formatting, 55

lines, *continued*
  inserting between paragraphs, 54
  specifying height and width, 55
linking web pages, 88–89
  See also hyperlinks
links, external, 18, 19
  See also hyperlinks
Link view. *See* Hyperlinks view (FrontPage Explorer)
listing
  images in FrontPage Explorer, 28
  web pages in FrontPage Explorer, 28
lists
  bulleted, 57
  numbered, 56

maps, hyperlink
  See also Hyperlinks view (FrontPage Explorer)
  moving, 16
  refreshing view, 18
  updating view, 18
  viewing, 14, 16
margins, frame, 131
marquees
  coloring background, 149
  converting headings to, 147
  creating, 146
  defined, 146
  deleting, 149
  editing text, 148

marquees, *continued*
  options for, 148
  width and height, 149
menu bar, FrontPage Explorer, 14
merging table cells, 104
Microsoft Excel, exporting web pages to, 31
Microsoft FrontPage, starting out, 5. *See also* FrontPage Editor; FrontPage Explorer
Microsoft Office, exporting web pages to, 31
Microsoft PowerPoint, exporting web pages to, 31
Microsoft Word, exporting web pages to, 31
moving
  data between table cells, 109
  hotspots, 76
  images between table cells, 112
  images within web pages, 64, 65
  text between applications, 47
  text between web pages, 46
  text within web pages, 46
multimedia, defined, 7. *See also* images; sounds, background; video clips

naming
  bookmarks, 87
  frames, 131
  web pages, 95, 96
  web sites, 8, 9

navigating web pages, 86
navigation bars, 167
Navigation view, 20, 28
news protocol, defined, 90
new web sites, creating, 8–9
numbered lists, 56

opening
   existing web sites, 6, 10
   FrontPage Editor from
      FrontPage Explorer,
      28, 82
   web pages, 38, 82–83

pages. *See* web pages
paragraphs
   as bulleted lists, 57
   formatting, 52–53
   indenting, 53
   inserting lines, 54
   as numbered lists, 56
   selecting, 53
passwords
   in text box fields, 175
   for web site access,
      190–91, 201
permissions, 197, 198–199,
   200–201, 202–3, 204
Personal Web Server, 8, 154
PowerPoint, exporting web
   pages to, 31
previewing web pages
   in browsers, 85
   in FrontPage Editor, 93

printing web pages, 92–94
Programs menu, 6
properties, web page, 29
protocols, Internet, 90
publishing web sites, 205
push button fields
   adding to forms, 182
   changing properties, 183
   defined, 173
   renaming button, 183
   what they do, 183

quitting FrontPage Explorer, 11

radio button fields
   adding to forms, 178
   changing properties, 179
   vs. check box fields, 178
   defined, 173
   naming, 179
recalculating hyperlinks, 19
Refresh button, 86
registration. *See* User Registration forms
removing. *See* deleting
renaming web sites, 196
replacing text
   using FrontPage Editor, 39–41
   using FrontPage Explorer, 33
resizing
   frames, 130
   hotspots, 77
   images, 63, 110, 112
   setting viewer options for, 131

resizing, *continued*
   table cells, 115
   text, 49
   video clip viewing area, 144
rich text format (RTF) files, 42
right-aligning text, 52
rows, table
   adding, 102
   defined, 100
   deleting, 107
   header cells, 121
   stretching cells, 124
RTF file format, 42

Save Results files, 186, 189
saving
   form data, 186, 189
   images, 96
   web pages, 95–97
Scheduled Image
   Component, 161
Scheduled Include Page
   Component, 162
scrolling, setting viewer
   options, 131
scrolling text-box fields, 173,
   176–77
searching for text
   using FrontPage Editor, 40
   using FrontPage Explorer,
      32–33
Secure Sockets Layer (SSL), 8,
   9, 205
security issues, 197–204
selecting text, 39, 53
servers. *See* web servers
SmartHTML, 154

sorting
   To Do List tasks, 22
   in FrontPage Explorer Folders
      view, 15
sounds, background
   file size, 140
   inserting, 140
   specifying when to play, 140
   whether to use, 140
spacing, table cells, 115
special characters, inserting in
   web pages, 43
special effects
   background images, 136–38
   background sounds, 140
   coloring background, 134–35
   marquees, 146–49
   overview, 133
   video clips, 141–45
spell–checking web pages, 34, 44
splitting
   frames, 129
   table cells, 104
starting FrontPage Explorer, 6
status bar, 79
Stop button, 86
storing web sites, 8
stretching table cells, 124
subheadings, creating, 50–51
Substitution Component, 163
Summary view. *See* Folders view
   (FrontPage Explorer)
symbols, inserting in web
   pages, 43

tables. *See also* cells, table
   adding, 101
   adding captions, 105
   adding cells, 102

The manuscript for this book was prepared and submitted to Microsoft Press in electronic form. Text files were prepared using Microsoft Word 97. Pages were composed by Stephen L. Nelson, Inc. using PageMaker for Windows, with text in Stone Sans and display type in Stone Serif and Stone Serif Semibold. Composed pages were delivered to the printer as electronic prepress files.

Cover Designer
Tim Girvin Design

Interior Graphic Designer
designLab
Kim Eggleston

Graphic Layout
Stefan Knorr

Indexer
Julie Kawabata

Register Today!

Return this
Microsoft® FrontPage® 98 At a Glance
registration card for
a Microsoft Press® catalog

U.S. and Canada addresses only. Fill in information below and mail postage-free. Please mail only the bottom half of this page.

1-57231-637-3A   *MICROSOFT® FRONTPAGE® 98*   *Owner Registration Card*
AT A GLANCE

_____

NAME

_____

INSTITUTION OR COMPANY NAME

_____

ADDRESS

_____

_____

CITY   STATE   ZIP

Microsoft®*Press*
Quality Computer Books

For a free catalog of
Microsoft Press® products, call
1-800-MSPRESS

BUSINESS REPLY MAIL
FIRST-CLASS MAIL   PERMIT NO. 53   BOTHELL, WA

POSTAGE WILL BE PAID BY ADDRESSEE

MICROSOFT PRESS REGISTRATION
MICROSOFT® FRONTPAGE® 98
AT A GLANCE
PO BOX 3019
BOTHELL WA   98041-9946